Salecology Unleash your Sales Superpower

Dear Jonathan,

Thank you for your friendship and support.

Best wishes

Darren Bezani

Darren Bezani & Jenni Bezani

Salecology Unleash your
Sales Superpower

Darren Bezani & Jenni Bezani

ISBN 9781914615702

A CIP catalogue record for this book is available from the British Library.

Published 2023
Tricorn Books, Treadgolds
Bishop Street
Portsmouth PO1 3HN
www.tricornbooks.co.uk

Salecology Unleash your Sales Superpower

Contents

FOREWORD 11

INTRODUCTION 13
The Evolution of Sales 14
Welcome to Salecology 18

Part 1 – The Psychology of Selling 23

THERE IS NO SUCH THING AS A 'NO BRAINER' 24
IQ vs EQ 25
Five Categories of Emotional Intelligence 27

FRIEND, PREDATOR OR POTENTIAL LOVER 32
Rapport 33
5 Biggest Mistakes in Building Rapport 40

OUR COLOURFUL PERSONALITIES 44
Jungian Theory 45
The Four Personality Types of Salecology 47
We are all four colours 55
Colourful Emails 57

SHUT UP AND LISTEN! 62
Emotional Drivers 62
Do you hear me? 64
It's not what you say! 66
It is not about you! 68
Accessing the subconscious mind 69
Finding the Triggers 71

Part 2 – Salecology through the Sales Cycle 73

LET'S TALK 74
Do your Research 74
The 3 Whys 77
Opening the Call 79
Initial Positioning Statements 80

LEAD THE CUSTOMER TO THE SOLUTION 85
Leading with the solution 85
Fabs to riches 87
Why ask questions? 91
Which is More important – Pain or Gain? 93

INFLUENCE THE MIND THROUGH QUESTIONS 98
Open or Closed Questions? 98
Do your questions engage the brain? 102
4Q Questioning 105
Metrics are more than ROI 112

PUT THE CUSTOMER INTO A BUYING MINDSET 114
The Value Proposition 115
Hypnotic Language 116
The Hypnotic Heartbeat 116

ADAPT SALES PRESENTATIONS TO MAKE SENSE 122
Filters and Representational systems 122
Brain Operating System (Cognitive Styles) 123
Dealing with larger groups 135

NEGOTIATE THE CLOSE 137
Wrong Reactions 137
Where is the objection coming from? 138
3 Step Approach to Objections 140
What happens to personality when it moves into negotiation? 144
Win/Win – I don't think so! 146

DEALING WITH PRICE 154
Price Concerns 154
Framing the price 155
Suspending belief 156

Part 3 – Building your Emotionally Intelligent Sales Organisation 159

HAVE I GOT THE RIGHT SALESPEOPLE? 161
What does Great look like in your organisation? 161
Assessing talent for the new world 168

HOW DO I BUILD 'OUR WAY' OF SELLING? 170
The Customer Journey 170
Mapping the Sales Process 171
Define the Knowledge, Skills and Behaviours 173
Playbooks and Game plans 174

HOW DO I COACH FOR HIGH PERFORMANCE? 177
Is it a Skill or a Will Issue 179
Do I need to tell people what to do! 181
Focus on the behaviour – not the results 184
Coaching Models 188
Final Thoughts 195

FOCUS GOES WHERE ENERGY FLOWS 196
What makes you likeable? 196
Storytelling 198
Beliefs and Values 200

FURTHER READING AND BIBLIOGRAPHY 205

INDEX 211

About the Authors

Darren Bezani MBA is the CEO and co-founder of Salecology. He has an extensive sales and leadership background, having led international teams and delivered sales transformation for all sizes of organisations including, start-ups, scale ups and as well as many global enterprises across US, EMEA and Asia Pacific. His research, work and training has been implemented in over 55 countries around the world and has been translated into 16 different languages.

Darren has a pragmatic approach to sales development and training and ensures that he identifies the elements that make a real difference, not the theory. He passionately believes that sales is an art, but every individual needs the science which are the tools and knowledge to develop their sales behaviours into an artform. He travels the world in search of the latest tools the high performers use to apply their art and influence people to say yes! He shares in this book some of the findings from psychology, neuroscience, linguistics, sociology, and the pragmatic applications of it across the sale, and how to build a sales organisation that achieves high performance.

Jenni Bezani is co-founder of Salecology and Chairman of Salecology International. Jenni is passionate about organisational success and driving growth. She believes the emotional imprint that we leave at every touch point in our customers and stake holders is the deciding factor of our success. Jenni has MBA from a prestigious European Business School and with over 25 years of experience transforming businesses across Europe, Middle East, America and Asia, she has seen the world of sales change dramatically over the years. Jenni has played an integral part in research, creating, developing and testing Salecology models and methodologies that are already used over 55 countries across the globe. Jenni has helped clients achieve many accolades for their development programmes, through 'Investors In People', the UK's 'National Training Awards', 'Global Awards' and the 'Personnel Today Awards' to name but a few. More impressively, she has supported her clients to triple new business, halve discounting rates and deliver double-digit revenue growth year on year. Jenni is a master in reprogramming people's brains and have had an amazing opportunity to meet and work with thought leaders from across the globe. She has coached royalty, movie stars, Olympians, sports professionals, politicians, business leaders and high performing individuals to be the best. Jenni passionately believes that as leaders, it is our responsibility to unlock our peoples' full potential for them to be the best at what they do. Jenni combines this knowledge in this book to bring to you a unique set of tools that can create the right energy, influence outcomes and get more people to say yes to you!

Foreword

As with the majority of salespeople, I fell into sales. My parents told me I needed to get a job so I found one – in sales. It's a job people take when they are trying to determine what they want to do in life. And as with the majority, I found out I was good at it, loved it in fact, and enjoyed the various aspects of it, the interaction, the creativity, the fun of the chase, influencing outcomes and of course the rewards, especially the commission and the things I could buy. What is interesting is that back on the late 80s, sales training and development was a little scarce to say the least. It was more sink or swim, watch and listen to others, copy what worked and drop what doesn't. Over the past 30 years a lot has changed in sales, and now we have all sorts of processes, technology, sales aids, and many organisations have broken down the sales roles to create teams of hunters (new business) and those who are more farmers (account managers).

Nowadays there are all sorts of great sales improvement training programmes out there. I am sure you have already been on some training, but here is the question – did it help? Over $45bn was spent on sales training last year alone, and over 80% of it failed to make an impact. That's because, as you'll learn in this book, knowing what to do is very different from being able to do it. Which leads to an age-old question – are great salespeople born or are they made?

We have spent the last 20 years looking at sales behaviour across the world and identifying aspects that separate good and great salespeople. We asked the question – does selling on the east coast of America work the same way as on the west coast? Or does selling in a Latin-based country work the same as a Germanic one; or if I am in China, does selling work in Shanghai the same way as in Hong Kong, or Australia vs New Zealand and so on? The answer is no! Cultural differences obviously have an impact as do personalities and processes. Do the top performers in those different areas therefore do things differently or are there some traits that we can identify that they all seem to have that makes them great?

The answer to that is yes. In today's world, the customer is more informed than ever, and they believe that whatever you are selling, they could probably buy it cheaper somewhere else. The person who typically wins the sale, is the person who builds the best connection and trust in the customer.

This is something that natural-born salespeople have intrinsically known and utilised to be great, even though it is unconscious behaviour. So in answer to the question, yes, great salespeople are born. However, great salespeople are also made and through our research and experience, we are now able to bring to you the facets that will enable you to adopt those principles into your sales repertoire and methodology.

Sales training for the best part has been more technical training, which is important; a salesperson must know their products and services, but the training they receive is not built around how to emotionally engage their customers and lead them to those products and services. Yes, people are taught questioning techniques, how to make an elevator pitch, how to objection handle and so on, but this is all taken from the position of fact and logic, but humans are irrational! Yes, the product may stack up, but they are not emotionally engaged enough into the value proposition or you!

So welcome to the *Salecology Unleash your Sales Superpower.* This book is broken into three different sections to help you build the tools and techniques that can help you and your organisation drive greater customer engagement, and learn how you can maximise your sales team performance and potential, achieving significant top-line revenue growth by emotional engagement, both of your sales team and your clients.

Introduction

To date, you have likely received a lot of Sales 101 training. That's great when you're just starting out, because just like every other subject on Earth, if you don't have the fundamentals down, you'll never be able to build on them. But a lot of sales strategies have gotten painfully outdated as we race onward into the third decade of the 21st century. More than ever, businesses are focused on customer experience to generate profit. The heart of every business is the customer. Now this is nothing new, but what I would like to challenge you with is, if everyone knows the customer is king, why are we still not nailing it in our sales?

There are lots of things that sales need to be successful. Processes for a start: how we find the customers, how we entice them, how we reach out, how we connect, how we move them through the customer journey, how we close – all that good stuff. We also need the infrastructure in place, and the tools to deliver the numbers that we thrive on. But fundamentally, the biggest weapon that powers the machine is the opportunity to look into the customers' brain; we need that insight into how they think and what drives their behaviour. Then that information has to be matched up with our own salespeople's' brains, thinking and behaviours. There are many factors influencing the connection that we can create with another person, the depth of conversation, and the productive outcome of that interaction. Without this inspection and understanding, our sales process will never be anything more than taking a shot in the dark.

If you've ever worked in any kind of business with multiple salespeople going after the same client base with the same opportunities, you see the same phenomenon. A few of your salespeople get the best results and the rest of them don't. Why is that? Are these guys just natural talents? Why are they so good at getting the deals? Or are they just good relationship builders, or persuaders or influencers? Do they know the products better, or the market, or do they have greater industry knowledge perhaps?

In order to understand and gain insight into why these things are happening, and why so many of our sales departments are still struggling, we had to take a look at the point of sales interaction from another angle.

Answering those questions turned out to be quite a bit more involved than we first thought. When we started digging into the concept and what the answer was, we found layers upon layers from several fields of science, and it was quite clear there is a lot more to sales and psychology – what we have termed **Salecology**. In order for you to have a successful sales organisation, your sales staff needs to use Salecology in every interaction with their customers. This is the only way you can get ahead of the competition in your industry and have a consistently effective and successful sales team.

So, before we get started, let's take a quick recap on the history and evolution of selling.

The evolution of sales

Bartering goods between individuals or groups of people is as old as humanity itself. Once our distant ancestors stopped following the herds of buffalo, woolly mammoths and deer and settled down to farm and fish, markets sprung up as the world's meeting place. As far back as 10,000 BC, cattle were a desired commodity, and those who raised them or herded them had the power to trade them for the things they needed most. There was a fixed currency for what cattle were worth. Little bartering is thought to have been done. Over the centuries, selling evolved and people came to value different things for different amounts based on their needs. Currency developed and merchants began to grasp the different values that products had for different customers based on their circumstances. The finely woven net had next to no value to the man who lived on a mountain, but to the one who lived next to the sea and fished for food and profit every day, it was worth a fortune! Selling as a profession is one of the oldest examples throughout time of people having specific responsibilities to negotiate and trade.

When the industrial revolutions took over in the UK and US (1760–1840), rapidly developing companies began using sales campaigns and other new business methods. This was also the beginning of the era of professional salespeople, whose main purpose was to travel around the country and persuade people to buy their products. What was the reasoning behind the concoction of this new way of doing business? Competition. The ability of factories to rapidly build products ramped up the competition. Suddenly things that had only been sold by one company for years or even decades could be purchased from several different suppliers. Suddenly availability was no longer the single most defining quality for customers when it came to purchasing a product. For the first time in history in many industries, the focus shifted from the company making the product to the customer buying it. Now that customers had multiple choices of where to buy from, companies had to up the ante on getting their company picked. The need for salespeople to talk up the products, list their positive qualities, broker a price and downplay what the competition was capable of, suddenly became absolutely essential.

This trend continued until the 1950s when the modern era of professional selling began. Technology had taken another huge leap forward with radios in every home and televisions rapidly joining them. People were driving longer distances to work and on road trips and saw billboards all over the country. Commodity selling took off, with manufacturers selling parts and products in business-to-business bulk orders. New techniques were springing up all over the industry like the good old 'bring and brag', 'show and tell', and 'spray and pray'. Marketing became the leader in how sales were enabled to customers. The five Ps – People, Product, Place, Price and Promotion – ruled the roost. Marketing was sales' new teacher, even though plenty of the students had no interest in being taught. Marketing in that era looked a lot like modern-day TV shopping channels: it was all about being a good persuader to your audience, even if it was something they did not necessarily need or want. Marketing departments were writing scripts for salespeople, teaching them how to demonstrate projects, telling them how to answer questions, teaching them good presentation skills, and tutoring them on closing techniques.

Fast-forward 20 years and the thought process change to say 'hang on a minute, would it be a good idea if we were to ask the customer some questions first, find out what their wants and needs are, and then show them our products?' It was the beginning of the Solution-selling industry. The customer's problems became the focus. If we were the ones to solve that problem, we were much more likely to make a long-term customer. This technique involved asking a lot of questions, even more listening skills, and conducting a 'Needs Analysis'. From there, we were into 'Features and Benefits' – pick the right features and benefits to highlight in order to close the sale. Stop me if this is all starting to sound quite familiar!

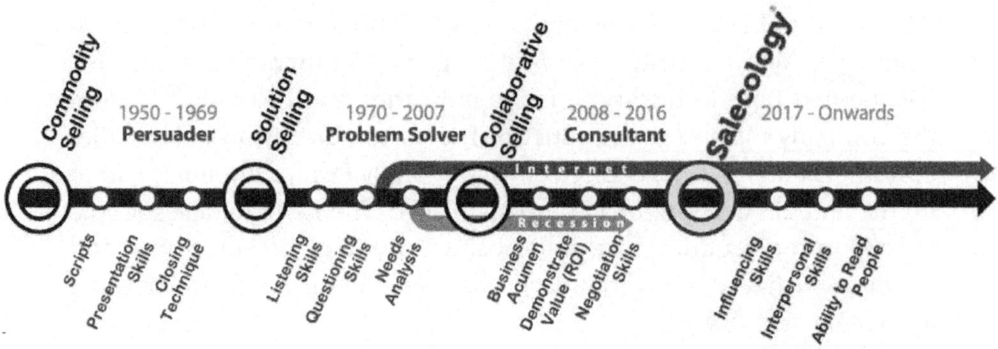

Technology finally started catching up with technique soon after the turn of the millennium, with the development of internet sales and ecommerce. The internet didn't really take off in earnest, especially as we saw the dotcom boom and bust in 2004, however the way people sold changed forever as we moved into 2007–2008 when the global financial crisis struck. In mere days for some people, a big chunk of their world collapsed with the bubble bursting on the US housing market and the precipitous drop of markets all over the world. People's retirement funds vanished in a heartbeat. Those approaching retirement age saw their savings drop by as much as 80%. Selling anything became a major challenge as most people and businesses slashed budgets and sign-off levels. Salespeople had to reinvent the wheel and did so with a more collaborative approach. Top performers in this era knew they had to break inertia in the customer accounts and 'Challenge the Status Quo' by bringing insight to a customer, challenging their thinking and most importantly to demonstrating a return on investment. Negotiation skills came to the fore during this period to win or retain the business!

A great outcome on this evolution to modern-day selling was that a more collaborative approach came through as organisations, and its people started to separate themselves with the concept of being a thought leader.

Something else changed over this period; people were taught to go compare! What's the first thing you do today if you want to buy something substantial or want to research a product you might be interested in? You look it up online, of course! Usually via Google or by simply punching the brand name into your search window. And why do you choose this method? Because a huge swathe of information that you'll need is available right there at your fingertips. You can compare and contrast one product with the next, get price quotes, read reviews, and it's all very convenient and very fast. For plenty of people, this is all they need. They trust their peers and what the colourful screen says enough to make a purchase. But of course, not everyone is like that, in fact when it becomes a considered purchase, people want and need to engage with other people.

The internet might give customers a lot of information, but there's more to making a sale than reading user reviews. People still go to retail stores and talk to salespeople in droves because they can offer unique things that the online store cannot, namely:

- The ability to touch/feel the product and see it outside of a monitor.
- The ability to get advice from a real person.
- The ability to potentially negotiate on the price instead of being locked into whatever the sticker tag says online (or spend hours trying to find a coupon).
- The experience of a live expert on the product and others like it.
- The knowledge of whether it's in stock or not; even Amazon is not fast enough to deliver merchandise instantaneously (yet).
- Customer service: no phone calls or online messaging, you've got a store with live humans.
- Aftercare: easily get the warranty or any other repairs done by bringing the product back to the store you purchased it from.

So, here's the problem, as we look through the evolution of selling, the sales have become more logical and data driven by providing business information and intelligence, return on investment metrics, and negotiating renewals and prices. But as you can see, the customer is more informed than ever, but what they really want is more emotional support in their purchasing, making sure they buy the right thing, from someone they trust. So there is a significant mismatch between what salespeople and organisations think they should focus on – product features and services – and what is really going to drive the customer to buy – emotional engagement.

Salespeople believe and have been taught they should focus on data, facts, market analysis, features, benefits and price. The problem is that this has already been supplied by the internet. What makes people buy, and buy from the salespeople in particular, is a totally different thing, especially in a world where product differentiation is becoming more and more difficult.

Welcome to Salecology

So this is where Salecology fits in. It looks at the sales methodology and the psychology of selling and how to connect with the customer in both logical and emotional ways. The journey of understanding how to impact and influence others has made us realise that there are lots of different sciences we need to dip into to understand how it works. In this book we have drawn insight from the fields of neuroscience, psychology, sociology, neurolinguistic programming and sales to analyse how people buy and what makes people say yes. Psychology reveals how personality and intellect affect behaviour; sociology shows how people respond in group situations and to social pressure and trends; neurolinguistic programming shows how to influence anybody anywhere through using the dynamics between mind, language and behaviour. Neuroscience has uncovered how the brain functions, both consciously and unconsciously, and the art of selling is to present and customise your message according to how the customer needs it.

This book is not designed to make you a sales psychologist, that's our job, but it is designed to share with you the magic that sits within it that will help you modify your sales style and approach to maximise your relationships with customers and how to influence their decision making. Having said that, below is a highlight of the different sciences that we will use in this book and how they can be used in various areas within sales and marketing.

Neuroscience

Neuroscience is used to develop our ability to influence decision making, the buying process, empathy, rapport, communication, the sales process and customer service.

Salecology reviews brain functionality to understand the signals that put people into a 'fight-or-flight' mode when prospecting, and to learn how to adapt different strategies for objection-handling or negotiating a sale. Neuroscience offers us an unparalleled viewpoint to enhance our understanding of both sides of the sales equation – i.e. the sellers and the buyers – and therefore achieve results that are mutually satisfying.

Areas included:

- Engaging customers in a conversation
- Buying impulses
- Selling impulses
- Reasoning and decision-making process
- The human brain functions
- High-performance state
- Thinking and decision patterns
- Building confidence in customers

Psychology

All buying situations contain both business process and personal psychology. Most salespeople emphasise the former. In this part of Salecology, we will show you how to adapt your selling style to the customer's personality type and deliver a great buying experience.

By understanding personality and human behaviours you will be able to create trust instantly and influence individuals on a different level. Using psychology in sales will satisfy both the rational and emotional parts of the brain. Think in terms of buying cycle, rather than selling cycle.

All human beings have the same mental triggers that drive actions. In order to influence and understand your customers, you need to know what those triggers are and how to utilise them in your message.

Areas included:

- Selling to different personality types
- Human behavioural patterns

- Buyer personas
- Using emotional intelligence
- Aptitude and intellect in complex sales
- Influence and persuasion techniques
- Overcoming price barriers
- Transactional analysis – leading the customer
- Buying triggers
- Storytelling

Sociology

We like to believe that we are immune to outside influences, but studies find that our surroundings play a key role in the decisions we make. Peer pressure affects aspects of everyone's life.

Salecology utilises the study of sociology to learn how to apply sales influence through trends, cultures and social networks as well as how to create the right atmosphere that will drive the customer to buy.

Selling to one or two people requires one set of skills, however by paying consideration to group dynamics, the sales professional will also be able to sell more successfully to organisations, boards, panels or decision-making groups.

Areas included:

- Atmospherics
- Impulse buying
- Trends and social pressure
- Group dynamics
- Playing the ego
- Presence and gravitas
- Relationship-building with groups
- Building sales messages
- Standing out from the crowd
- Board room dynamics

Neurolinguistics

Language is an amazing tool that determines how people interface and communicate with others. By using specific language that brings out certain feelings in people, sales professionals can develop emotional connections and trust with their customers that are necessary in sales interactions and marketing.

By understanding the dynamics between mind, language and behaviour the salesperson will be able to adapt their selling style to communicate with customers in a deeper, more meaningful way. Discovering how people receive and interpret information will enable them to ask questions and present solutions that will ignite their customers' passion. This part of Salecology also teaches how to change people's state of mind. This can be used to put the salesperson into a high-performing state, or to put the customer into a receptive or buying state.

Areas included:

- Creating instant rapport
- Modifying sales language
- Building a high-performance mindset
- Questioning techniques
- Influence and change the buyer's mindset
- Getting customers to open up
- Body language
- Hypnotic language
- Powerful emails and communication
- Sales presentations

Sales

Using each of these above sciences in isolation (for example only using persuasion theory) will bring you some – but limited – success. It's only through the seamless integration of all five study areas that we can truly combine head and heart together both consciously and unconsciously in the way we act and sell to all prospects and customers.

Salecology brings all of this together within all aspects of sales to exert an unprecedented influence on customer decision making.

Throughout the chapters of this book you will learn how to modify your sales approach utilising a combination of the above. It might not always be obvious which parts of science you are using, and that doesn't matter, but we want to show you the magic and how you can maximise your relationships and success with using Salecology.

Part 1 – The Psychology of Selling

This section of the book is designed to give you a solid background in linking psychology and how it plays out in sales. If as many as 95% of decisions are made in the emotional irrational part of our brain, it is useful for you to look at the Salecology and how the science comes into play at different parts of the process. Don't worry, it is not just theory, we will help you identify how it plays out and how to harness it to build engagement and influence throughout the sales cycle.

There is no such thing as a 'no brainer'

Most people learn in school that the left side of your brain controls the right side of your body and vice versa, but those two hemispheres also control different parts of how your mind works, specifically how you think things through and make decisions. The left side of your brain gives you the capacity to think in words. It performs linear thinking and sequencing and is concerned with logic and facts when making a decision. If you excel at maths, thank the left side of your brain which is where mathematics is processed. Meanwhile, the right side of your brain is concentrating on feelings and visualisation.

Your imagination is birthed from the right hemisphere, along with things that you know are true but you can't explain – like your intuition, your sense of rhythm and your ability to create artistically. This breakdown of functionality in your brain was first discovered by Nobel Prize winner Roger W. Sperry, a neuropsychologist, back in the 1960s. By being more creative, the right side is also the more emotional.

So what? If we take the concept of the left and right brain and apply it to sales, we can consider two parts of the sale:

1. The structured and logical sales proposition; and
2. How the customer feels about it.

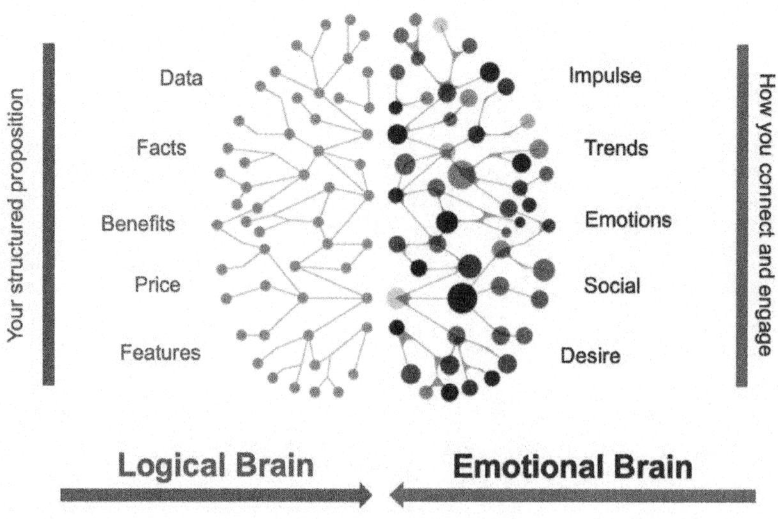

IQ vs EQ

IQ, or intelligence quotient, is used as a way of measuring a human's intelligence. Do you have average intelligence, are you below average or above average, or are you a genius? Most subjects in schools and colleges are designed to teach knowledge and score your ability of recalling that knowledge or applying it, and then they grade you to tell the world how clever you are (or not). Some kids excel at this and other kids excel at other attributes of school, such as sport, acting, crafts, singing and so on.

In sales, a lot of importance is placed on building a 'strong value proposition'. Does the product make sense, does it meet the customer's needs, does it add value and deliver a return on investment? In fact, in the previous chapter, the evolution of selling demonstrated that almost all sales techniques taught to date are based on rational thought and logic. The 50's style of the persuader was to present the product and tell you all about it (facts), the solution seller will conduct a 'needs analysis' and present features and benefits (facts), and the collaborative salesperson demonstrates that return on investment – again all based around the rational left part of the brain. But if it all adds up and makes sense why doesn't everyone buy?

A good example of this was the banking fiasco in the UK from 2012 through to 2019. The banks were found to have mis-sold an insurance product called Payment Protection Insurance (PPI) and had to repay everyone who was mis-sold. About 64 million policies had been sold from 1990 to 2010, and as they had been tagged on the back of loans, credit cards and mortgages, the chances are you didn't know you had bought one. Making a claim for a rebate was not difficult, but less than 10% of potential claimants made a claim in the first five years. Lots of firms sprung up across the country to offer help for people to make their claims, or to make the claims on their behalf. Here is the typical value proposition:

> *I will write to all the banks and find out which ones owe you money, I will also find out how much they owe you. I will then tell you, if you then want me to, I will make the claim for you, get all the money together, and then send you the money. No risk, no fee. Bearing in mind that you haven't done this over the last five years, and are probably not going to do it before the time runs out, how about if I do all the work you pay me 20% of anything I get back for you.*

I'm paraphrasing but you must admit a strong proposition, a 'no brainer'. All the upside and very little downside – a commission. But the majority of people hung up on the sales calls. Why? I'm sure you have similar stories about sales deals that you have worked on or observed; the return on investment demonstrates every reason for them to go ahead, it ticks all the boxes, but for some reason they don't buy.

The answer lies in the emotional, irrational part of the brain.

Everywhere you look there are some interesting deals to be had, a myriad of products to save or give you more time, save you money, or make you money, make you a better life, increase your health and so on. But something inside us acts as a compass, leading us towards or away from certain deals. I don't mean because the offers won't help, it means am I really interested? Is this something I want to invest my time and effort on even though it is financially or physically beneficial?

This emotional, irrational part of the brain forms part of our subconscious mind. It is not conscious thought but more a 'gut feeling'. Harvard Professor Gerald Zaltman identified that up to 95% of all decisions are made in this unconscious part of the mind. Marketeers have been trying to tap into this for generations – product placement on a shelf, colours used on packaging, names of products – all designed to conjure up an emotion or affiliation with the product, but salespeople have been somewhat lacking at identifying this key to unlocking an emotional engagement into the deal.

With the latest research into neuroscience, combined with the learnings from NLP (neurolinguistic programming) we can develop better ways to engage the customer into the sale. Yes, the value proposition must stack up, if your products and services don't meet the needs of the customer then you are not even in the race. Having a product that meets the need is the pre-requisite but it only gets you to the meeting, it is not going to win the deal.

The successful salesperson needs emotional intelligence, also known as the emotional quotient (EQ), which encompasses a person's ability to express, control, evaluate and identify emotions. EQ is widely known to help people become better leaders and team players since they are able to understand the emotions of the people around them better. The term was first coined in 1985 by Wayne Payne in his doctoral thesis 'A

Study of Emotion: Developing Emotional Intelligence'. It found its way into the popular vernacular in 1995 in a book by Daniel Goleman entitled *Emotional Intelligence – Why it can matter more than IQ.*

As you can probably deduce, EQ has become far more important than IQ when it comes to sales. Our ability to read other people's emotional signals correctly and react accordingly can mean the difference between a huge order and a polite – or not so polite – dismissal. When your EQ is on point, you understand the people you are trying to sell to, specifically what motivates them and how they want to be sold.

Five categories of emotional intelligence

Psychological researchers have broken EQ down into five categories, all of which are essential to being a great salesperson in the modern landscape. The five categories include:

1. **Self-awareness:** Self-awareness is your ability to recognise your own emotions as they happen. You might recall the old saying, 'Never let them see you sweat'. That is a great mantra for sales. In fact, you want to do your best to keep any negative emotion out of your facial expression and body language because you're not the only one who can pick up on those kinds of non-verbal clues. If a client sees you get angry, upset, depressed, annoyed, your sales meeting is going to change direction pretty rapidly. There's nothing wrong with having those feelings; they are part of what self-awareness is all about. But when you have them, you need to evaluate them and manage them in order to make sure they don't interfere with your ability to make a sale. Also, contrarily, they can be used to influence the thoughts and feelings of your customer. The two components of self-awareness are:
    - **Emotional awareness**, which can be summed up as your ability to recognise not only your emotions, but also their effects on you and others; and
    - **self-confidence**, which is one of the most essential parts of sales. Being confident and sure in your capabilities and what you can do will greatly improve your EQ.
2. **Self-regulation**: When you feel a negative emotion, you can use a number of techniques to determine how long you stay in those states. We're all going to get angry, anxious or frustrated over the course of

our jobs as salespeople; you'd have to be the greatest salesman of all time, or have no feelings at all, not to. Self-regulation necessitates learning and practising techniques that can not dampen the emotions themselves, but the way they are able to control you and throw you off your normal emotional state. Things like meditation, exercise and counting your blessings are all well-regarded practices to mastering self-regulation. The five components of self-regulation include:

- adaptability
- trustworthiness
- self-control
- conscientiousness; and
- innovation.

In terms of your emotions, innovation refers to your ability to be open to new ideas while adaptability means you can handle change with flexibility. Your self-control keeps you from indulging in too many disruptive impulses, and your trustworthiness is the core of your standards for your own integrity and honesty. Both of these traits are also essential in a successful salesperson. Treating your customers with honesty and integrity instead of trying to milk them for all their worth is essential to long-term success.

3. **Motivation:** Different salespeople have different motivations. For some, it's all about the bottom line, for others, it's the feeling of truly solving problems and satisfying customers; while for others it's about being the best. Whatever your goals are, make them clear and use a positive attitude to get there. Positive thinking is an incredible resource for salespeople, one that is reinforced every time you succeed.

   The core components of motivation are:

   - optimism
   - initiative
   - commitment, and
   - drive (for achievement).

   Those all blend together in the best type of salesperson, the one who believes that every client can become a customer and who pushes themselves to maintain their own level of success, not one put forth by a sales quota or an overbearing manager! Commitment involves aligning your goals with the ones laid out by your company, and initiative revolves around being ready to seize opportunities as they come your way.

4. **Empathy:** The heavyweight champion of EQ for salespeople is their ability to be empathetic. Being able to not only recognise how people think and feel, but also to be able to 'put yourself in their shoes' and feel those same emotions. Some people are naturally empathetic, and when they choose a career that highlights it, they are amazingly successful. For others, empathy is a lifelong learning process that involves lots of skills that salespeople also covet, such as the ability to listen and respond, not simply waiting talk, and the ability to gain someone's trust utilising non-verbal gestures and body language.

   When you can read the signals that someone else is giving off emotionally, you can naturally pick the right signals to send back to them. This is so crucial in dealing with a client, especially for the first time, when you are trying to ascertain their needs and motivations and respond accordingly. An empathetic person is excellent with service orientation, developing others, leveraging diversity, understanding others, and has high political awareness. Service orientation is the lynchpin of sales: it allows you to anticipate, recognise and meet your clients' needs. Understanding others allows you to identify and understand the feelings behind their wants and needs.

5. **Social skills:** If you have good interpersonal skills, you're likely to go a lot farther in your life and in your career. With the ability to look someone up on the internet and be connected to them via a phone call or video conference literally seconds later, people skills have never been more important. If you have a high EQ, you have a much better chance at understanding, negotiating with, and empathising with someone, even if you're only connected by a video screen halfway around the world.

   The most useful of these social skills are:

   - leadership
   - communication
   - influence
   - change catalyst

- team capabilities
- collaboration/cooperation
- building bonds; and
- conflict management.

Whether or not your client knows it, you're always taking the leadership position in the relationship to inspire the client and guide them towards a certain decision. Many of the rest of these skills are among the bread-and-butter tools you need to be an effective salesperson – communication to send clear messages; influence to effectively persuade a client; bond-building to nurture strong relationships now and in the future; cooperation, so that you and your clients can work together on mutually beneficial deals; and being a catalyst of change, which is often needed for clients to stop settling for the status quo and get them on board with a new way of thinking, a new technology or simply a new plan.

EQ is the core principle of Salecology. When you begin to truly understand how your customer thinks, you move that much closer to forming the kind of relationship that will last for the long term and benefit both parties again and again.

Therefore the real drivers of why customers buy, sit not on the logical side of the brain, but more on the emotional/irrational side. These include things like:

- impulse
- trends
- what people are saying is cool
- feedback and reviews
- internet comments
- sheer desire
- ego (make me look good); and
- mood.

That means that everything emanating from the right side of the brain is something that can be convinced, influenced, induced or reinforced to make a buying decision. To be a top performer, you must learn how to influence and connect with individuals on the emotional side of their brains.

That walking, talking brochure salesperson – which is what the internet basically is – only fulfils the logical requirements of a human decision to buy something. But those requirements are not even one half of the picture.

The era we are now living in requires us to become more emotionally and socially intelligent. You need to be able to speed read and connect with individuals on both the physical and emotional level. In doing so, you can create a deep-level rapport and a lasting trust that will empower you to influence and lead the customer towards a purchase while remaining genuine and authentic throughout the process.

In order to achieve that tall order, you will need a better understanding of how your own brain works, something we've already touched on above in the comparison of right brain vs left brain functionality. But it goes beyond an anatomy lesson. You'll need to understand behavioural patterns and emotional triggers, and how to unlock these using language, non-verbal interactions and influencing techniques.

Friend, predator or potential lover

Let's start at the primitive end of relationship building. Whenever you meet someone for the first time the brain takes the minimum amount of data and looks to decide whether they are:

Friend – is this person good for me? Something about them makes me warm to them and I tend to move towards them.

Predator – is this person bad for me? Something about them makes me wary and I tend to back away from them.

Potential Lover – remember I am talking about the primitive part of our brain here, and it is totally subconscious, but something might trigger this!

Indifferent – I physically see you but nothing gets triggered. You are totally indifferent to me.

The majority of these decisions are made instantly on the first of your senses – visual. How you look, how you're groomed, dressed, shoes, etc. all play a part, and then it's combined with your body language, what do I see and how does it look to me. Then the flood of all your other senses kick in, such as what you hear i.e. what is said and more importantly how it is said.

Other senses get triggered as well including smell, which can have a positive or negative impact, and of course the infamous greeting which can prove awkward. Let's take the simple handshake which often tells us a lot about a person. But in different societies the handshake can mean different things, for example in China the strength of grip needs to be light, whereas in Germany it needs to be strong. In Morocco you finish the handshake off with putting the back of your hand to the back of theirs or in Rwanda you are more than likely to grab their forearm instead of the hand. These greetings can be different all over the world and can invoke different emotions:

Bow – *Cambodia, India, Nepal, Laos, Thailand and Japan*
Air kisses (on the cheek) – *France, Italy, Spain, Portugal, Latin America, Ukraine and Québec, Canada*

Rub noses (sometimes forehead) – *New Zealand*
Touch (bump) noses – *Qatar, Yemen, Oman, United Arab Emirates*
Hand on heart – *Malaysia*
Stick your tongue out – *Tibet*

The first aspects of the middle part of your brain, often referred to as the reptilian brain, is where all the sensory data is received by the thalamus and distributed to other parts of your brain for deciphering. As it forwards on the data it sends a quick pulse to the amygdala which controls that fight-or-flight response. It is here that determines that Friend or Foe response.

As we have advanced a few million years, we are less conscious of this fight-or-flight response and this primitive part of our brain is not triggered so often, unless of course something comes our way such as a salesperson trying to sell me something. Does it invoke a predator-type response or are you open to engage as you think they are more friend? Or do you engage because you need to buy something but are on guard and will keep your barriers up to defend yourself against any attacks?

I have often ask people what they do when they know a salesperson is coming to call. They have invited the salesperson to visit, for example a window glazing salesperson is coming to measure and quote for new windows. Do they somehow – consciously, or otherwise – prepare to protect themselves against a pitch? Most respond that they do prepare themselves to 'not allow the person to sell to them' but rather just give a quote. They withhold data, not allow the salesperson to get into the pitch or somehow try to tell them to go and measure and quote. In essence, keep them at arm's length. Why do you they do that? Well they don't want to be sold to, or they don't want to be somehow pressured by the seller. It is a fight-or-flight response.

Rapport

To overcome this fight-or-flight response we need to talk about rapport and its importance in building connections with customers.

Everyone wants rapport. Rapport is that feeling when two or more people are totally connected to one another. Think about when you meet someone for the first time, what's the first thing that happens? Usually it is some form of questions, like how are you? What do you do?

Did you see the game at the weekend? Or you share stories or exchange knowledge and so on. Why do you do that? People ask this question to try and find somethings in common with one another and start to build rapport. Rapport is therefore that feeling of commonality and is the spark which brings people together.

Rapport can be started and built by a common interest like the industry you are both in, where you went to school, a sport you like, an area of the country you are familiar with, or simply something that interests or amuses you both.

Rapport plays a big part in the whole sales cycle:

Prospecting – we can open opportunities with people as they are more willing to engage.

Discovery – people will divulge more sensitive information during the exploration stage of the sale.

Presenting solutions – people are more willing to listen and engage with sales presentations, and more susceptible to collaborate.

Gaining commitment – people are more empathetic in negotiations and look for win-win outcomes and more likely to say yes.

How to build rapport

One of the key elements of determining who people see as a 'friend' is understanding what makes people like one another. In general, people tend to like people like themselves. If you are like me then I like you, if you're not like me then you're different and that's where problems arise.

Some salespeople think that the key to building rapport is by having an outgoing personality and being able to engage people socially like you would at a cocktail party – the sort of effortless conversation starters that for some come as second nature and others find to be as baffling as brain surgery and astrophysics. But if that were the case, only the extraverted personality types among us would be successful at building rapport, but we know that is not the case.

When different types of behaviours come out, some people might warm to them while others will be quite repelled. Let's take a simple dynamic of pace of voice in a sales call where a fast-talking salesperson is engaging with a slow-talking person. The slower talking customer might feel that this fast-talking salesperson is trying to hide something and that's why they are talking so fast, or they are trying to confuse them, and therefore might consider them untrustworthy. Equally a fast-talking customer might become extremely frustrated at a slow-talking salesperson, think they are labouring on the point and want them to hurry up and get to the point of what they are saying.

Volume is another trait to consider with verbal patterns. Those loud talkers can come across obnoxious to some, while others may warm to it as they are demonstrating passion or power. Equally, a quiet talker could come across as polite and considerate while others find them too timid and passive.

The point here is that one style does not work; if you're like me then we tend to get on quicker and rapport gets built much faster then if you're different. If I'm that outgoing social person, and you are an outgoing social person, then we will get into rapport quickly, if you're the quieter more introverted person I might be too loud or excitable for you.

When people are in rapport you will see that they are totally connected, on the same wavelength or in sync. Their brains are literally connected! They seem to know what each other are thinking or feeling, they can even finish each other's sentences. The body language also shows when people are in rapport as they have a huge tendency to physically copy one another's body movements. Both could be nodding, smiling, sat with their legs crossed or leaning forward and so on. The people become so in sync that they end up matching and mirroring each other.

Matching and mirroring

Early adopters of NLP in sales have often used the terminology of mirroring. In Salecology we utilise some of the early content of the founders of NLP, Richard Bandler and John Grinder, and split this into two components: matching and mirroring.

Matching is matching the customers verbal communication style and ensuring that what you say and how you say it matches their style.

- Pace
- Tonality
- Pitch

- Volume
- Cadence
- Phrases and jargon
- Brevity
- Word preferences

Mirroring can establish rapport with individuals being mirrored. Mirroring the other person's non-verbal gestures make the person feel a stronger connection to you.

- Body language
- Posture
- Gestures
- Facial expressions
- Proximity
- Standing or sitting position

These are extremely important in the way we connect with each other in all sales communications including phone, email, messaging as well as face-to-face meetings. It is our ability to demonstrate that we are on the same wavelength by using our language to match and trigger connections with people and use mirroring to imitate some of their movements and actions.

Before we continue and share with you some ways to build rapport quickly, I want to emphasise that rapport, matching and mirroring is a subconscious behaviour. People do not do it purposefully, it just happens and therefore if you start to do it consciously it will feel strange, but in order for it to be successful you must remain authentic you. If you overplay matching or mirroring the other person will become consciously aware that you are doing it and this will not just break rapport but can result in a total loss of trust in you.

Doing your research before you meet can help you look for areas for rapport building. This can involve checking them out on social media, looking them up and connecting on LinkedIn, or reading their bio on their company website to see what nuggets of information you can glean from it. Of course, that luxury does not exist for every salesperson. If you work on a showroom floor and await customers strolling through the front door, you can't exactly ask them for a link to their LinkedIn page and to hold on for 15 minutes while you do your research! In those types of situations, being quick on your feet and mentally aware will get the process started. Here are some great ways to build rapport with your newest clients.

When you engage directly with a potential customer, you want to match their body language and communication style as closely as possible to make them feel comfortable with you. You can start this process by emulating how they are holding themselves. For those working in retail, watch the customers' methods of walking into and around the store. Are they fast paced or slow paced? The walking pace can often match their speaking pace, i.e. they are in a hurry or they are taking their time. You can match and mirror that pace when you approach them which will do wonders to engage quickly and get a better response.

If you are both sat in an office and they sit with their legs crossed, you should do likewise to mirror them and show you are paying attention. As described earlier, you should also match their verbal patterns such as pace and volume. If they are slow and deliberate with their half of the conversation, you should do likewise. If they are deliberating over every word they share with you, don't act like you're running a sprint when it's your turn to talk, be as deliberate. Match their pace of conversation as well as you can.

Remember, there are limits to all of this. Matching and mirroring isn't about copying everything they do. It is more subtle than that. It's not about mimicking every behaviour – they touch their nose, you touch your nose; they cough, you cough; they blink, you blink. Keep the body language in check and keep your voice emulation overall to a believable level. I was in Houston, Texas once on a business trip and needed to drop into an electronics store to buy some equipment for a sales workshop. Of course, the salesman had no idea that I was a salesman too, so I had to hide my smile behind my hand when he began matching my way of speaking, right down to my British accent! As one might imagine, hearing my accent reimagined through a Texas drawl did not quite have the rapport-building effect the salesman was hoping for, but kudos to him for going all in to make the sale!

Manners matter

Your mum did not drill into your head about the power of 'please' and 'thank you' for the 18 years you lived at home just so you could forget it all once you reached adulthood! Using your manners and being friendly is the way to let people know you're a professional from that very first moment of contact.

Be curious and be interested

Being a people person is more than just smiling when they walk through the door and a firm grip on your handshake. You also need to take a genuine interest in the customer and learn as much about them and what they're looking for as you can. Be curious! Everyone has a story to tell of why they're looking to buy and what brought them to this point. Learn more about them and get a reading on their pulse. The more information you have, the easier it is to identify what solution you can provide for their problem. Not only that, but also realise that the more you talk to them, the more likely you are to discover people they know or work with that could also benefit from your product or solution. Instead of trying to wrap up a sale as quickly as possible, realise that building rapport with a client can lead to easy sales when they recommend you to friends, family and co-workers based on your easy-going demeanour and willingness to help. Also, if you are genuinely curious, the questions you ask will uncover so much more from the customer, who will feel your interest and warm to your genuine nature.

Don't force it!

If someone comes in wanting to get right to the price negotiations and signing the paperwork, don't try to slow down their momentum by asking them who their favourite band is or querying if they watched the game at the weekend. Rapport comes naturally and as time allows it to. It might be that your new client has no interest in chit-chat until after they've gotten into the deal and determined you know what you are talking about. Mirroring their no-nonsense behaviour in the first instance and 'being all business-like' will build rapport and you will see at some point the customer will begin to open up. That's the point you can start to probe a little bit and learn a bit more about them. Not everyone trusts a salesperson, and some will be wary of 'letting their guard down' for fear that you'll talk them into something they aren't looking for by laying on the charm. Find the opportune moment, match and mirror to start building that rapport and then support and challenge in a polite way if you need to slow them down a little.

Be a succour

A play on words is always helpful. Succour means to assist, help and provide aid. When your customer talks about you to other people, you don't want them referring to you as 'the salesperson'. You'd much rather be referenced by name or worst case as 'The lady that gave me amazing insight and help choosing the right deal for me' or 'I've got a buddy down there who always hooks me up'. How do you accomplish this feat of rising above the role of just merely being the 'salesperson' and into your client's circle of trust? By never making it about the sale! You'll build so much more rapport by casting yourself as someone who helps solve a problem not someone after their money. You need to position yourself as the person who can get them what they want and need, solve their problem, and make the impossible become possible. No one ever wants to buy a solution; they want to solve an issue they have. Think about it, when was the last time you thought to yourself, I am looking for a solution!

Don't forget about cadence and follow-up

If you meet someone at a party or some other social event and the two of you hit it off like old friends, would you say goodbye to them at the end of the night and simply never attempt to see them or speak to them again? Of course not, that's not the way the world works. When we meet someone interesting, we have unlimited ways of connecting with them to stay in touch, whether it's a phone number exchange, email, instant messenger, social media connection, or simply a promise to go grab a bite to eat or have a cup of coffee. The same holds true as you build a relationship with a new customer. A follow-up phone call or email should be automatic. You also need to ensure that not every interaction is a sales interaction. It never ceases to amaze me how many salespeople don't follow up, quickly. When you have had an engagement with a customer, the best time to get back in touch is often within 24 hours. The experience and engagement with you is still fresh in their mind and then getting another contact from you outlining the conversation, highlighting the next steps or thanking for the order goes a long way in building and extending the rapport.

If you want a more meaningful relationship, make sure some of your communications and correspondences are not related to the sale. Sharing information that you think might be of interest will go a long way in developing rapport. An email link to an article with 'I saw this and thought you would enjoy reading it' tells the customer you are so much more than 'the salesperson'. Or a call just to check in and a catch-up – without any alternative agenda.

Five biggest mistakes in building rapport

Just as there are ways to master building rapport, there is a definitive list of what to avoid when trying to do so. These are some of the most common stumbling blocks you'll run into in your quest to achieve perfection with every single client that comes your way. No matter how on point your game is, there are going to be some customers who are not going to be easy to build rapport with, and some who will have no interest in doing it at all. This can be a tough pill to swallow for salespeople who want to succeed with everyone, be on a first name basis with all of their clients, and want to get a Christmas card from each and everyone to thank them for their marvellous business.

At some point, no tactic is going to work for a tough client who doesn't want or need to 'connect'. Better to go through the sales process the way the customer wants than to risk annoying them and losing the sale because you're obsessed with breaking down barriers and building rapport. Here are the five biggest mistakes you can make when you try to force someone into building an unnatural rapport with you.

1. **Being too friendly:** Too friendly can be construed the wrong way and it can just be plain annoying for a customer. You might be the most interesting person in the world, but that does not mean that every customer wants to be your new best friend. In fact, rapport does not have to equate to friendship. Rapport can be built by two professionals who have an understanding of one another's needs, and work together to build out the solution. Some of the best clients you'll ever make might be people who you establish a pattern of supply and demand with, and when they need your help, it's a quick phone call, text or email consisting of nothing more than a delivery date, an order size and a brief thank you. That sort of rapport can be just as powerful and satisfying as having a five-minute conversation without the need to spend 15 minutes sharing photos of your children and talking about the latest from Wimbledon.

2. **Spending too much time in deep rapport not wide rapport:** Having a conversation with someone you can either discuss a wide

range of subjects or you can get deep into one particular area. Hence the difference with deep rapport and wide rapport is whether your rapport is built in one particular topic or you have expanded the things you talk about. Within sales, it is typical to start by building a narrow deep rapport because you are obviously focused on helping the customer fulfil their unmet needs. One of the challenging things for some people to do is take a leap of faith and change the topic of conversation to something else and start to build wide rapport. This doesn't need to be too difficult though. Firstly, changing locations when you speak to the customer. By speaking to people from different mediums and location, e.g. calling from the car or calling at a different location on a video call, their brain recognises things are different and it starts to build a level of familiarity and trust in you. Secondly, storytelling is a great way to move onto different topics and usually the customer responds by sharing a similar experience or story with you. Storytelling brings more personality into play – yours and theirs – and builds wider rapport.

3. **Being distracted**: This can be increasingly noticeable in our modern era of go-go technology where everything demands a look at your phone, a swipe, a like, or a thumbs-up. So many people have such a hard time disconnecting from their technology that they can't stop looking at it, even when a potential customer is sitting right in front of them! If you've ever tried to have a conversation with someone who can't stay off their smartphone, you know how incredibly annoying and irritating this sort of behaviour can be. How can a tiny screen compete with a living breathing person right next to them or right there on the phone? The truth is that it shouldn't but nevertheless it does.

   Some of us get so addicted to our screens that we don't even realise how much we are utilising them. This leads to divided attention, a lack of eye contact and missing critical words, clues and clauses as we flit our attention back and forth to our smartphone or some other electronic distraction. Smartphones aren't the only distraction – your own sales systems can create distraction, especially if you're not prepared. I have lost count how many times I have observed a salesperson who has a customer live on the phone and are busy trying to read (discreetly) some notes on the computer while they are talking, or that showroom salesperson who is busy looking at other customers and not giving the person in front of them their full attention.

4. **Trying too hard:** If you've ever been around someone trying to get into a relationship, especially when on the dating scene, you already know what this looks like. A shower of unearned compliments, laughing at every joke they make like they're Ricky Gervais at the Golden Globes, dazzled by any suggestion they make on virtually any subject, and so on and so forth. Going overboard in an attempt to impress someone does not work once you are past 10 or 12 years old, and never works with someone smart enough to know that you have ulterior motives. When it's obvious that you're grasping at straws in order to connect with someone, the feeling they get is that you're desperate. For most people – customers, bosses, colleagues and otherwise – that's a huge turn-off. In a sales context, some customers will sense the desperation and use it against you to leverage the best possible offer. Either way, it's not a good look for you, and definitely won't build any rapport any time soon.

5. **Communicating at the wrong level:** We've talked about being organic and natural when you first meet people. The challenge comes at different stages in your own lifecycle and also who you are communicating with. The psychologist Eric Berne developed the idea that people can switch between different states of mind depending on the situation. He termed this as Transactional Analysis, and we see this behaviour play out in many sales scenarios where people can take one of three roles:

   Parent – This is the voice of authority towards someone. It can be controlling, nurturing or critical. The critical parent can be harsh and sometimes aggressive, whereas the nurturing parent may be seen to be more of a rescuer and looks to sooth others.

   Adult – This state is more open, rational and quite often focuses on the here and now. When communicating from an adult state people tend to be more respectful, listen to others and are willing to make compromises where appropriate.

   Child – This state can come in two varieties; typically in a sales scenario the adapted child state conforms and acts to the wishes of the customer in order to please. There is also a free-child state which is more creative, spontaneous, and playful. The sales manager may see this state more often than the customer.

It is considered the best working level is adult to adult. Both parties listen and respond, they are respectful of each other and therefore tend to reduce conflict. However, the challenge comes at different stages in your own lifecycle and how you initially perceive you customer and miscalculate each other's role. You may be intimidated by their wealth, job title or status and therefore move to a child state and become too subservient to the customer and look for approval from the 'parent' or continue to ask the customer what they would like to do next.

An example of this would be if a customer came to you complaining of their recent purchase, using very belittling language, determining that this mistake had been made due to your lack of listening and told you that they were going to escalate this, speaking to you from their critical parent state, intending you to then reply from your child state, e.g. you will be very apologetic, begging them not to take it further, responding with anything that strengthens their authority in the situation.

The way to deal with this is to respond from an adult state or parent state. Transactional Analysis believes that responding from an adult state is potentially the best option because it accommodates the parent state and would likely mean the customer would also move to an adult state, which is the best, more healthy and respectful place to be.

The opposite could also happen, you may be arrogant to your own superiority, position and/or knowledge and take an elevated view and treat others incorrectly. I have seen this walking into some premium fashion stores where the salespeople are looking at you to determine if you can afford to be in their store! You never know what a customer might need or want, how much or how little they might spend, or what their background is. That's why rapport is such a vital tool here. If you only go by your first impression without extending the hand, giving a smile and asking those simple questions, you'll likely jump to an unsound conclusion and fall into the trap of selling to the person you think is in front of you, instead of the customer who is there.

Our colourful personalities

You can type 'types of customers' and get three million results with three million different theories about how people are classified: by where they are from, by what they do for a living, by how they spend their money, even by what their favourite type of food is. It all makes for interesting reading to be sure, but at the end of the day it all comes back to the one defining point: 95% of all decision making is made in the irrational and emotional brain. How people think and what personality traits they possess are going to define how they shop, how they process decisions, what they spend their money on, and how they want to be sold to.

That last factor is the Golden Goose because more than anything, as we discussed in the last chapter, people like people who are like themselves. If you're talkative and social, you're going to veer towards the sales rep who gives off the same kind of vibe. If the salesperson wants to tell you all about the technical data, and walk through extensive details, they make some good points, but their dry delivery is going to bore the life out of you and cost them their commission.

There's a world-famous saying that you should 'treat people the way you want to be treated'. That's a marvellous concept for everyday life, but it does not fit the bill when it comes to being a salesperson. If you're shopping for a new car and you're a stickler for the details, you're going to do an incredible amount of research and compare and contrast every single detail of every car on your list before you even step foot into a showroom. When you do make contact with a representative of the dealership, you're going to want to confirm your research about the fuel economy, the safety rating, the extended warranty, etc. from the type of person you hope knows even more about the vehicle than you do. But if the salesperson who gets paired up with you is more interested in telling you how fun the car is, how cool you'll look driving one, and how he sold one to a famous rock star last month, you're going to shut down quickly and likely take your business elsewhere.

OK, so not all entirely new, we have discussed this already in terms of building rapport. The salesperson has failed to recognise what kind of person you are and how they can adapt their own actions, words and non-verbal communication to sell to you in the method you want to be sold. To fast track building rapport and make it easier to communicate with the variety of customers, we can group certain types of behaviour into personality types. By understanding how they work and adapting your style accordingly you will be able to build instant rapport with your customers and become that trusted partner they want to do business with. But how can you quickly tell these types apart and how do you sell to each one of them? Glad you asked!

Jungian theory

A pioneer of modern psychology, Switzerland's Carl Jung founded the field of analytical psychology and was a frequent collaborator of Sigmund Freud, although the pair's work went in different directions during the 1910s. Jung's breakthrough work came when he borrowed the concept of archetypes from anthropology and began to break down human personalities into different categories such as extraversion and introversion, and even more important for our purposes, the idea of persona – an element of one's personality that comes to the forefront for "reasons of adaptation or personal convenience". Jung called these 'masks', as people put them on depending on the situation.

Over time, Jung's grand work were his 12 archetypes of personality, which he based off four main ideas and assigned each a spot on a colour wheel, something that we have brought forward into our Salecology personality study as well. Jung's four central ideas that all the archetypes derived from are that people's main trait is to do one of the following four tasks:

a. Provide structure
b. Take a spiritual journey
c. Connect to others
d. Leave a mark

His 12 archetypes along with the things they seek are:

1. Ruler – Control
2. Artist – Innovation
3. Innocent – Safety
4. Sage – Knowledge
5. Explorer – Freedom
6. Outlaw – Liberation
7. Magician – Power
8. Hero - Mastery
9. Lover – Intimacy
10. Jester – Pleasure
11. Everyman – Belonging
12. Caregiver – Service

The assigned colours to each of the 12 archetypes were; Ruler and Artist reside in blue; Innocent and Sage in green; Explorer a greenish yellow; Outlaw yellow; Magician and Hero in shades of orange; with Lover and Jester belonging from pink to red to purple, respectively. The colours derive from the four temperament theory first suggested by the legendary Greek physician Hippocrates, who lived from 460–370 BC. He described the four fundamental personality types as sanguine, choleric, melancholic and phlegmatic, based on the even older concept of the four humours which were liquids that our bodies were made up of. Ancient physicians believed that when the four humours were out of balance it led to people getting sick, and having different emotions, moods and behaviours. We have taken the notion of the four humours and mixed it with some of Jung's finest work to adopt our own colour scheme to the four types of personality traits represented by Green, Blue, Orange and Red.

Before we get to those four types and what each one means, let's speak a bit on our process. We build on Jung's work of the notion of extroverted and introverted peoples as one of the two axes on which our four personality types are built.

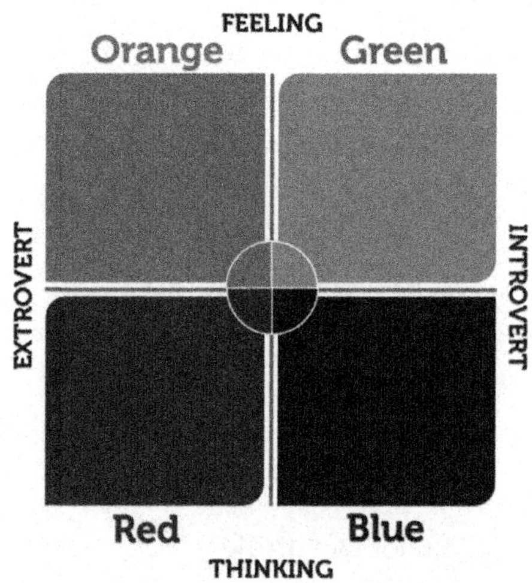

At one extreme, you have the extroverts of the bunch. These people are talkative, involved, outspoken and bold. Their focus is outward and they get their energy from other people. You'll often find them needing to talk to put their thoughts together, something we call 'Thinking Out Loud'. If there's a party going on, they are either controlling the music, taking every other turn on the karaoke machine, or playing bartender to connect with as many people as possible while still getting plenty of words in edgewise. Your Red and Orange personality types fit into the extroverted mould.

On the opposite end of that slide are your introverted folks. They tend to be quiet, observant, thoughtful, reserved and reflective. Their focus is inward and they are much more likely to think through their answer before they talk. At the same party as the one mentioned above, you'll find them in a smaller group, or perhaps even outside, engaged in quiet conversations with an intimate group people. These are our Green and Blue personality types.

On the other axis is how we make our decisions, and we break it down into two central ideas: thinking and feeling. The thinking end of the dichotomy make and take decisions based on facts and logic. They are ruled by the head and you will find they are more focused on the task and getting it done. The Blue and Red personality types are at the thinking end. The other end of the dichotomy is feeling and, although interested in the facts and data, makes and takes decisions based on their emotions, and often basing those decisions by being considerate and caring about other people. Where the thinking preference was more task-focused, this end of the spectrum is focused on the relationship and people. Our Orange and Green personality types fit in here.

The four personality types of salecology

So we've got the process down, what are the results?

Salecology Orange

The Orange personality type is extroverted and makes decisions based on personal values and empathy for the situation. They are interactive, optimistic, sociable, dynamic, friendly and creative. When someone who is an Orange personality type engages with you, you'll see that they are friendly, open and honest. There is fun in the buying process and the Orange loves to be engaged, involved and entertained throughout. Spontaneous in nature, don't look for detailed plans and in-depth analysis, they prefer the big picture idea, to be involved and be creative with it. This personality type could find themselves impulse-buying a little more than any of the other colours.

With this personality type you will see different aspects about what they can be like on a good day, for example when they are working well with others, and also on a bad day, when sometimes strengths become overplayed.

On a good day Orange can be:

√ Creative	√ Innovative	√ Resilient
√ Curious	√ Inspiring	√ Visionary
√ Energetic	√ Gregarious	√ Motivating
√ Optimistic	√ Self-Starter	√ Dynamic

On a bad day, these strengths can be overplayed and come across:

√ Impulsive	√ Disorganised	√ Exuberant
√ Scatty	√ Overly optimistic	√ Impatient
√ Changeable	√ Excitable	√ Unrealistic
√ Indiscreet	√ Frantic	√ Unfocused

Selling to Orange personalities

Connecting When connecting with an orange customer remember to make eye contact and utilise open, positive body language. Use personal words and pronouns, i.e. what are 'we' looking to do, or what should 'our' solution look like. You need to be sociable with this type of customer to connect with them.

Exploring Orange customers are interested in the big picture as they will have a vision of what they are trying to achieve. Two things need to happen during the explore stage. 1: you need to field your questions more about the future than dwelling on current problems or issues. 2: provide structure to their thoughts, as they possibly haven't. Look for personal meaning in the answer to the questions, not necessarily logical reasoning.

Demonstrating Make sure your proposal is delivered in a lively manner. Utilise an interactive style and get them hands-on wherever possible. Ensure you reinforce the future aspects of the product or service, and that it reinforces their vision. Don't ignore the details but stick to those features that they want and need, and demonstrate how and why this would look good for them.

Commitment Oranges don't want a blow-by-blow account of the T&Cs, or a breakdown of the bill. They will be interested in the overall cost and how soon they can have it. Objections or issues will appear as slight hesitations, and many will not be voiced directly. Look for these signs and call them out.

Remember that Oranges are the most impulsive buyer. If you are selling on logic and rational thought, you could well lose them. If you emotionally engage them, you have a great chance of the sale.

Salecology Red

The Red personality type is extroverted and makes their decisions based on the facts at hand. They are bold, efficient and focused. Their style of shopping is both fast-paced and action-oriented. They are far more likely to try and take control of the environment, even if they have never bought the product or service before. They might seem extra assertive, or maybe even a little bit aggressive, but that's just the way they come across, who they are, and how they behave, so do not be intimidated. You do not want to beat around the bush with a Red personality, you should definitely cut right to the chase as they are likely to make a decision quickly if they can, although be prepared to negotiate because they will also want the best price. Appearing flippant or hasty will get you rebuffed, and above all make sure you're correct in whatever you pass off as facts. If you're wrong, they're not going to cut you any slack.

Red personality on a good day:

√ Fast	√ Bold	√ Intuitive
√ Decisive	√ Efficient	√ Logical
√ Action-orientated	√ Assertive	√ Direct
√ Focused	√ Dominant	√ Demanding

Red personality on a bad day, when these strengths are overplayed or felt by others:

√ Intolerant	√ Controlling	√ Dictatorial
√ Driving	√ Abrupt	√ Angry
√ Overbearing	√ Domineering	√ Dismissive
√ Aggressive	√ Demanding	√ Impatient

Selling to a Red

Connecting When connecting with a Red customer remember to mirror their confident, straight talking, brash approach. Use fewer personal words and pronouns, i.e. instead of your usual 'we could' or 'our solution' use words like 'the solution'."

Exploring Reds have a strong ego about them and feel like they know everything. In the exploring phase ensure you put them into a process and ask them for a step-by-step rundown of the situation. Hone in on the facts and ensure you garner any key impacts. Don't labour on any points, but don't let the client stop you from getting some of the information either.

Demonstrating When demonstrating your proposal/solution to a Red, ensure that you're animated and that your presentation is short and to the point. Think bullet points. Replay the data gathered in the explore phase to reinforce why you are proposing various points of your solution, talk about the future and what could be.

Commitment Remember that Reds love to take a decision. They don't want to delay something they can sort out now. For Reds, they like to be asked for the order so utilise a step-by-step approach, explain to the customer the next steps and what happens afterwards, e.g. 'so if you can place you order now, the next thing that will happen is ...'

Be prepared to haggle. Reds love to test the salesperson both throughout the sale but also at the crunch point of booking. They will want to have at least a small win, so ensure you have something up your sleeve when that time comes.

Salecology Blue

The Blue personality type is introverted and makes decisions based on thinking things through. They are factual, objective, structured and consistent. They practice due diligence in everything they do, and are very intrigued by the details and theoretical concepts. All of that hard data might make them seem stuffy or even a bit cold, but that's just part of their personality. It's all about them getting it right. They want to explore and understand everything, and are perfectly willing to take their time doing so. They need to explore and understand and take their time. The details are paramount to any endeavour they undertake. The last thing you want to do is rush them; they require structure and specifics. Unlike your Orange personality type, the Blue is only worried about the here and now. Save the big picture stuff for someone else.

On a good day the Blue personality can come across:

√ Realistic	√ Analytical	√ Adaptable
√ Practical	√ Problem solver	√ Detailed
√ Factual	√ Objective	√ Logical
√ Pragmatic	√ Independent	√ Structured

On a bad day:

√ Too Serious	√ Detached	√ Defensive
√ Insensitive	√ Unemotional	√ Critical
√ Impatient	√ Blunt	√ Righteous
√ Cold	√ Cynical	√ Perfectionistic

Selling to a Blue

Connecting When connecting with a Blue customer type, remember to speak quieter and more purposeful. They prefer an indirect style with little challenge and place great importance on the sincerity of your approach. Pause when answering questions or giving information, and allow time for reflection. Be confident, use more closed body language and shorter sentences.

Exploring Blue energy will not be rushed in any stage of a sale. Use your questioning techniques to focus on identifying the cause as well as the pain, and extend it into the solution areas. Gain concrete evidence, not just anecdotal feedback, you will need it later in building the solution. Ask for step-by-step information, utilise 'what' and 'how' questions, and get into practical elements and applications. Focus on the logical implications of the specifics, don't guess – ask!

Demonstrating In demonstrating your solution, replay the facts before showing the feature. Utilise phrases like 'you said …' to show that you listened and are being pragmatic. Do not make statements that you cannot back up. Show the data and include evidence where possible. When talking about benefits or return on investment, use precise numbers or explain your workings if necessary.

Commitment This type of customer loves a process and structure. When looking to gain commitment utilise a step-by-step approach, explain to the customer the next steps and what happens afterwards, e.g. 'once you place your order the next thing that will happen is …' Do not incentivise a blue for a quick decision, if you could give the margin away then why haven't you already included that in the price. When overcoming objections, take time to understand the objection, ask for more information or data before responding.

Remember that Blues love facts and logic, and operate in a pragmatic, here and now, world. Big picture, intuitive and creative stances can frustrate this buyer as they prefer details, plans and structure. They will want to test your knowledge, weigh up the objective evidence and follow a pattern of logic – if this, then that. The Blue customer wants to get it right, they work at a steady pace and have little requirement for interpersonal connectivity; they especially distrust loud, outgoing salespeople.

Salecology Green

The Green personality type is introverted and makes decisions based on feeling. They are considerate, supportive, reliable and trusting. Greens have a very strong set of values and ethics. What other people think of your product can be almost as important to them as what they think of it. They are helpful and empathetic and want to know what other people will want to do with your products or what they use them for. Assisting others is key for these folks. They don't care how much you know about the product, they want to know how much you care and if you are able to empathise with them. Greens won't be rushed into taking the decision, but will gather the information and combine that with past experiences to come to their answer.

On a good day the Green personality is:

√ Conscientious	√ Trustworthy	√ Conventional
√ Practical	√ Methodical	√ Loyal
√ Compassionate	√ Empathetic	√ Organised
√ Caring	√ Diplomatic	√ Supportive

On a bad day, the green personality could sometimes display the following:

√ Cautious	√ Defensive	√ Slow
√ Reserved	√ Perfectionist	√ Procrastinating
√ Quiet	√ Obsessive	√ Change-resistant
√ Stubborn	√ Resistant	√ Risk-adverse

Selling to a Green

Connecting When connecting with a Green, remember to speak softer (not soft) with a slower calmer pace. They prefer an indirect style with little challenge and place great importance on the sincerity of your approach.

A gentle handshake will be more appropriate than a firm one, good eye contact is important to build trust but not too much as to intimidate. Remember for a green personality, you need to show them you care so be prepared for small talk and to share something a little more personal.

Exploring Green energy doesn't like to be rushed and when confronted by a fast-talking salesperson, may try to control the process by becoming stubborn. Use your questioning techniques in a less forthright manner, focusing on feelings and impacts on both the buyer and others around them. Ensure the questions and discussions are meaningful and demonstrate empathy to build trust. Gain concrete evidence, not just anecdotal feedback, you will need it later.

Demonstrating Although you may be very clear on the solution, don't tell Green the answer. They enjoy mutual problem-solving. When presenting the solution, ensure you use their words and play back how it helps both them and others. Using logical and rational statements will add credibility and continue to build trust and hearing how others have implemented the solution will also add credence to your proposal.

Commitment Getting Green customers to say yes will come down to the question 'do I trust you?'. Green likes to avoid risk, so building the relationship through the sales cycle is imperative. Helping Green through the buying process, rather than selling to them is the key to closing this sale. Overcome objections with factual answers as well as storytelling.

Remember that Greens come across as agreeable and welcoming and have frequent displays of modestly and accommodation. This behaviour does not constitute that they are a pushover though, they can be cautious and hesitant when making decisions, reluctant to commit quickly and often avoid change. They want to ensure you care about them and their situation and want to establish that the decision is right before taking it. Look for more content, data and information about them and their needs, because more often than not they will involve others in their decision making.

We are all four colours

The theoretic explanation of selling to four different types of customers is one thing, putting it into practice is entirely different. It will take a lot of practice and a lot of work, but what you will eventually be doing to cater to each of these four distinct colour personalities is to emulate what Jung first hypothesised when he coined the phrase 'persona' – which literally means 'mask' and for Jung meant the mask we wear in public to put across a certain image of ourselves, a certain role we are playing at the time. It is nothing sneaky nor dishonest, we all do it. If you are a married mother of two who works out with friends before going to the office and visits your mother in a rest home every Sunday, you've already taken on several personas – wife, mother, daughter, workout buddy, co-worker and employee – without even realising it. These are all slightly different versions of yourself that you subtly alter when engaging with a person who knows you primarily in that role.

Changing your own colour as a salesperson to sync up with the customer's colourful personality more closely must remain 'authentic you'. We don't want you to lose your personality, simply modify some of your behaviour to build better rapport and connections with the customer. The key to remember is that we have all four colours within us.

Sometimes we need to be Red – action-orientated, focused and driven; sometimes we need to be Orange – social, creative, chatty and engaging; sometimes we need to be Green – empathetic, caring and supportive; and sometimes we need to be Blue – diving into the detail and typing our reports. Just think about your everyday world in sales, you use all four colours throughout your role, Blue when working on customer database updates (CRM), Red when engaging that drive, goal-setting and competitiveness, Orange when picking the phone up and being highly interactive, and Green when taking time to cheer each other on and have those customer care calls.

Opposites don't attract

Another cliché that you hear a lot is opposites attract. It's important to note that these colours are called preference colours. Some of them give you energy and some take more energy. For example, if you are extroverted, being with and around other people gives you energy, while spending lots of time on your own can drain your energy. Therefore you have a preference for one over the other.

As an example, if I have a preference for Orange, I love engaging with customers, chatting with them, getting involved in creative problem-solving and brain storming, having the dinners and after-work drinks and so on. This super charges my batteries and therefore I am more likely to want to do that more then some of the other things, such as Blue things – typing up my quotes, working on slide presentations, doing my CRM updates, submitting my expenses. I can do it, but it drains my batteries and I might find I keep interrupting my Blue work to quickly chat or engage with someone (to give me energy).

So we have all four colours, it is just that we have a preference for one, or quite often on the border of two, over the others. What is interesting in the colour personalities is where you need to focus more attention to your opposite colour.

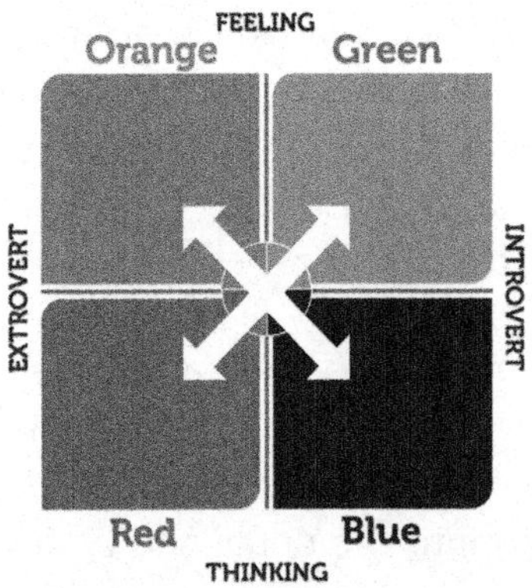

As a Red, you have things in common with Orange, you are both extroverted and like to engage in interaction and open dialogue, and you have things in common with Blue, you both like the data, base your decisions on logic and are focused on the task at hand. The colour you have least in common with is Green and therefore you will need to adjust your style the most to accommodate this.

It's the same for Orange and Blue as opposites, as an Orange you have things in common with Red, extroverted behaviours, and things in common with Green, both focused on people and relationships, but least in common with Blue. With Blue you will have the harder challenge of adjusting your style to accommodate theirs, and vice versa.

As a quick cheat, you can look back at the 'Bad Day' words for you and your opposite colour. This is how each of you would be likely to see each other.

Colourful emails

You can adjust a lot of your sales communication and style based on the colourful personalities. How to act on the phone, how to be in a face-to-face meeting, on a video call and on email. Below are some ideas on how to adjust your email based on your customers' preference colours.

Subject line

The subject line of an email has one job – to get the customer to open the email. There are many different conversations about this but taking a psychological approach is a quicker tool to help your customers to open the email and be excited to read on. Ethan Boldt, in his 2009 article in IDM, describes six principal motivators they believe impact open rates of direct mail; fear, exclusivity, greed, guilt, need for approval and anger. Tapping into any one of these emotions will have a direct impact on open rates.

Another option is to ask a provocative question that will engage your audience and again drive open rates. Statements like 'Transform your sales performance in 14 days' sounds punchy and clever, however the brain questions this, and disregards it as sales speak. Changing it to a question will build intrigue and get more opens: 'Is it possible to transform your sales performance in 14 days?'

We can look at both these points, and also add an additional dimension if we know the customer's Salecology personality colour. This will allow the email subject line to be more personal and more targeted. Below are some hints and tips based on personality colour.

Orange	Oranges enjoy personalisation, utilise their name and focus on the fear of missing out or exclusivity. '[Name], only 100 widgets left – last chance to order.' Optimism and creativity can also spark an email open: 'Where could you be this time next week?'
Red	For Reds, you can play the ego, such as making them the decision maker. Use phrases like 'Action Required: …', or a question looking for a response, '[insert statement] is this right?'. Greed also works with Red – 'Growth opportunities now revealed for business leaders.'
Green	Greens have a passion for supporting others. Use their name and ask for help or advice: '[Name], can you help me with this?' You can also use anger or a sense of moral injustice: 'Startling secrets that healthcare doctors are keeping from you.'
Blue	Blues are logical and data driven. Use a mentally challenging question that will create intrigue – 'Is it possible to compare x with y?' Also use statements for Blues which are factually based: 'Important information regarding …'

Greetings and opening the email

Greetings are an important part of an email. Many people use the typical 'Hi x, I hope you are well' or a variation on the theme. Although this email small talk is friendly enough, it is often overlooked and ignored by the recipient. There are lots of alternatives that you can use to engage the recipient, and for some personalities, getting straight to the point is better than any small talk version.

Direct, straightforward Reds and Blues as an example would definitely prefer emails that skip pleasantries and quickly address the point. More sociable relationship-oriented Oranges and Greens usually prefer the more personal introductions. Making one small adjustment to the opening can have an amazing effect on how the recipient reads and responds to the rest of the email.

Addressing the recipient is also something to consider in your email. Have you ever received an email starting 'Dear Sir/Madam', or 'To whom it may concern'? Chances are you ignored the rest of the email or letter. Psychologically, we consider being addressed like this means the email is not meant for us, almost as bad as misspelling our name. The email salutation is another aspect we can craft based on personality, adopting a formal approach or an informal, more friendly style.

Personality Type	Your approach	Techniques
Orange	Personal and informal	Enjoy a more informal tone and a good use of 'Hi' and a first name will be more than enough. Utilise a little small talk and make it fun. 'Hope you've had your morning coffee' or 'It's Friday, hope you have some cool plans for the weekend'.
Red	Formal and straight to the point	You can drop the 'Hi' and go straight to first name, or if they are new contacts consider use of 'Hello' and both names. Cut the small talk but you could use a simple 'I know you're swamped so I'll be brief'.
Green	Friendly and informal	Small talk is useful for Greens and ensure you keep it authentic. 'How are things in London?', 'Hope you are keeping cool during this hot weather'. If you are already connected, feel free to ask something more personal such as 'How is your dog Coco dealing with it?'. This changes the dynamic of the email considerably.
Blue	Formal and structured	Although Blue is formal and structured, they are still human and like to be engaged. Drop the small talk, utilise a 'Hi' or 'Hello' followed by the name. Sometimes a 'Dear [full name]' works very well, but drop the 'Mr/Mrs 'for new contacts. If you have met before, feel free to point it out 'We met at ...'.

Email content

Email content is quite varied, in one moment it could be as short and pithy as a text message and in others it can be pages long. Choosing how much content is too much or too little can be the challenge. Utilising the Salecology colours enables you to consider this is terms of the recipient's personality and build your content accordingly.

Oranges and Reds, for example, value brief, effective emails, while Greens and Blues prefer longer emails that establish trust. As in the subject and greetings pages, Oranges and Greens prefer a more casual tone where Reds and Blues prefer a more formal, business-like language. Emailing an Orange with a lengthy, data-filled email will guarantee that it is not read, Blues might be more engaged, but no one wants to read a novel via email.

Below are some hints and tips for different colour personalities:

Personality Type	Your approach	Techniques
Orange	Colour, graphics,	With Oranges, be forward thinking, big picture, inspirational. Use pictures and graphics, if possible, colour slightly larger font and don't labour on too many points. Keep it relatively brief. Utilise the word 'we' in terms of working together.
Red	Bullet points, action-orientation	With Reds, use charts or graphics, focus on action, be clear on what you want from them, use bullet points, tangible metrics, and face validity on all statements. If this is for information only, you should not have sent it! Use 'you' in language
Green	Photos, empathetic language	With Greens, build an emotional connection, be supportive – it's not about them but about others. Use examples and case studies, demonstrate empathy, use clear steps and pathways to make life better for others. Utilise 'we' in your phraseology.
Blue	Tables, attachments, links	With Blues be logical, informative and objective. Use research and data statements, cut down the length by use of attachments and add additional resources. Use third person language, i.e. make reference to 'the business'.

Closing the email and call to action

Just as you spent time ensuring that you start things off in the right manner, you also want to ensure you part in the same way. The call to action is what your email has been leading up to after all. This can either be a simple next steps, or if it is a prospective email you obviously want them to contact you or go to a specific landing page as part of your sales sequencing. Either way, utilising the personality colours allows you to provide the best chance of gaining the response you want.

Personality Type	Your approach	Techniques
Orange	Be positive and excite	Oranges want to be involved and usually want to get started straight away. Use an upbeat tone in the CTA and include them in it. 'I'm really excited to get this moving forward and meet with you, how are you fixed for tomorrow?'
Red	Ask for permission or tell what happens next	Reds want to move things forward and take action. Your CTA should be coming straight out with either a question or tell them what you want. 'The next step is for you to agree the above so we can …' or 'Does this work for you?'.
Green	Make it about other people	Greens are driven by supporting others so include this in your CTA and sign off. 'I appreciate your help on this and hopefully we can set up a time quickly to save your team any more issues. Are you free on …?'
Blue	Make it the next logical step, and include a list of actions	Although you have sent data and attachments etc., you never know if it is enough. Your CTA for Blues could continue to expand on this. 'Based on this information and data, the next step would be for us to get together and review the following: add a list of things you would like to cover off.'

Finishing the email with a sign-off is equally as important as the start of the email.

Here are a couple ways to continue the rapport:

- **Regards** – an old favourite, no offence received, but then again no extra credit either
- **Best wishes** – a good blend of friendliness and formality makes it safe bet
- **As ever** – good for people you've built a relationship with
- **Thanks in advance** – considered by some email apps to get the biggest response
- **I appreciate your help** – powerful sign of appreciation

Shut up and listen!

You might have heard the saying, made famous by Tony Robbins, motion drives emotion. My thinking from a sales context is more 'emotion drives motion', which means that a person's emotions are going to determine a whole lot of their decision making. That 'gut feeling' we all have at times is usually just our emotions letting us know what we really want, even if it's not what our logic centre tells us is what we need.

Your customers' motivations are driven by their emotions, and if you can tap into those emotions, you can get a very clear look at what is driving their mindset and what is going to trigger them to want to engage with you, or in looking at your product or service. However, if you are doing all the talking, then you can't listen to what is truly important to your customer, and it is not about your products' features.

Emotional drivers

You may often look for sport and hobbies outside of work to connect with the customer and build rapport, which is great, but in the workplace your customers have a number of emotional drivers that determine what they are working on and what grabs their attention. Some customers have career aspirations and are looking for ways to move up the corporate ladder, some are trying to build their personal brand as a subject matter expert, while others feel it is their responsibility to keep the organisation on a steady path and safe from risky decisions.

The eight emotional drivers

Arthur Carmazzi, in his book *Architects of Extraordinary Team Culture,* defined eight emotional drivers that help answer why people do what they do, and what their drivers are for doing it. He brought them into eight key aspects:

Belonging	a sense of belonging, either with people or with a cause
Security	that feeling of being safe and in control
Diversity	doing different things and a mix of variety in your life
Challenge	personal development, learning, stepping out of the comfort zone

Recognition	being recognised for your achievements, and for your virtues
Achievement	to finish things and progress forward
Excellence	self-satisfaction and pride in the things you do
Contribution	feeling of contributing and making a difference

In his book he points out that not all drivers are equal, and each person will have primary drivers and their level of commitment to certain tasks and projects and the mix of these drivers will have a direct impact on the person's motivation.

Work-based drivers

Knowing your customers' emotional drivers enables you to be selective in your engagements and look for ways to trigger these emotions through your correspondence, value propositions and negotiations.

Here are some examples of emotional drivers and triggers:

Innovation & change	**vs**	**Traditional & conservative**
They want solutions to be new, creative and innovative		Interested in solutions that are tried and tested, follow a well-trodden path
Aspirational	**vs**	**Comfortable**
Aspiring to move up the career ladder or they may be new into an organisation and want to make their mark		More comfortable and stable in their role and not motivated by what others think
Leading the business	**vs**	**Consensus driven**
Taking decisions and being seen as someone who makes things happen		Being inclusive in decision making and gaining team consensus is a real motivator
Groundbreaking	**vs**	**Conventional**
Groundbreaking inventions and brand-new ways of working, trail-blazer		Inspired by bringing in best practice, proven to work in their industry
Subject matter expert	**vs**	**Breadth of influence**
Burning desire to be the best, or an authority on the subject matter, set the standard for others		Focus on broad coverage and influence across the business

It is not that these triggers are individual ones, it is more of a combination of some of the above, e.g. the person could be aspirational and keen to move up the org chart, wants to be seen to drive the business forward and be an instigator of change.

Spotting emotional drivers

Emotional drivers are not easy to spot straight off and are more subconscious behaviours. Some of the aspects you may see from your online research include, are they publishing articles on social media and news forums, do they 'like' certain articles, what groups do they belong to and so on. Absence of these can also be indicators. If you know previous organisations they worked for, length of time in the current role, previous projects, why were they brought into this project, or why this project, again these provide you with lots of pointers and you can start to intuitively get a sense of some of the drivers.

Once you are engaged with them think about the questions you ask: do they help you understand more about what is driving them? The answer to that will come down to whether you shut up and listen to what they are really telling you, or are you just waiting to talk?

Do you hear me?

Nothing builds emotional engagement better than listening. If you feel someone is truly listening to you, how do you feel? You feel that they are there for you, they are paying attention to you, they are interested in what you have to say, they get you. So, listening, being present in the moment, builds greater connections between people. Funnily enough the opposite is also true, nothing breaks the connection than feeling like you are not being listened to. You feel ignored, frustrated, angry even, when the person you are talking to completely misses the point, or their body language indicates they are not listening.

It is actually a lot harder than it seems in today's world, where everything surrounding us is designed to distract us, to tune out of everything else and give the person we are with 100% of our concentration and stay interested.

Add on to that the fact that you are also a salesperson and you are supposed to be talking with the customer and selling to them, so even when they are talking, you are busy trying to think of the next question or be ready to tell them how you can meet their needs.

Five types of listening

Before getting into listening for your customers' emotional drivers let's take a moment to look at five different types of listening.

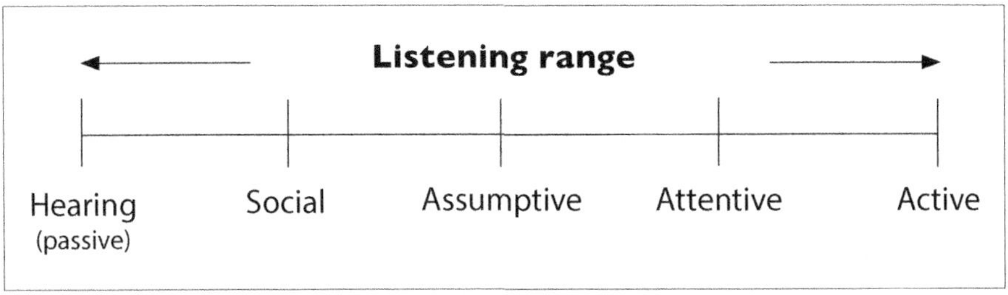

Passive listening

You probably remember getting your hearing tested as a child, either in a school setting or at a physician's office. They put on those headphones and have you raise your left or right hand, or click the button, to correspond to the sound you hear in said ear. We call this passive listening; it is the lowest form of listening and is simply a verification that you can hear.

Social listening

Imagine yourself at a crowded party or at a large dinner table with multiple conversations going on at the same time. You tune in and out of different conversations and join in at various moments. Equally, sometimes when you are at home you put on the radio or TV for background noise, and every so often you may hear something interesting, your ears prick up and you'll tune in to hear what's being said, or hear your favourite song, and then tune out again. This is called social listening.

Assumptive listening

Potentially the most annoying type of listening, and one that salespeople can fall into the trap of. Assumptive listening is in fact almost an oxymoron; the person might ask a question and already assume they know the answer. Those assumptive listeners have a bad tendency of cutting people off before they answer with phrases like 'I know what you're going to say' or, somehow even worse, answering the question for them. Assumptive listeners also might ask a question, and rather than listen to the answer, they are waiting to talk, or follow up with the next question, so they can dive in their bag and pull out the brochure.

Attentive listening

Once we get to attentive listening, you have a person who is listening to the other person. They are paying close attention to what is being said and demonstrate that to the other person by potentially noting down some of the points and capturing the data, maintaining some eye contact, their body language provides confirmations like nodding their head at regular intervals, and they are responding with some verbal affirmations such as aha, OK, right, yes.

Attentive also means that they listen and respond with follow-up questions, and ensures the person feels like they are being listened to as they are engaged in what they have to say.

Active listening

For a lot of people, the 'attentive' listening above was what they had been taught as 'active listening', i.e. listen and respond. Active listening takes a lot more work as rather than listening to what the customer is saying, the focus of being active is to ensure you are listening to the story and trying to ascertain why the story is the story.

It's not what you say!

Back in the 1971, in his book *Silent Messages*, psychology professor Albert Mehrabian of UCLA identified that: there is a significant difference in how much meaning can be placed on the various aspects of what people convey when communicating with one another.

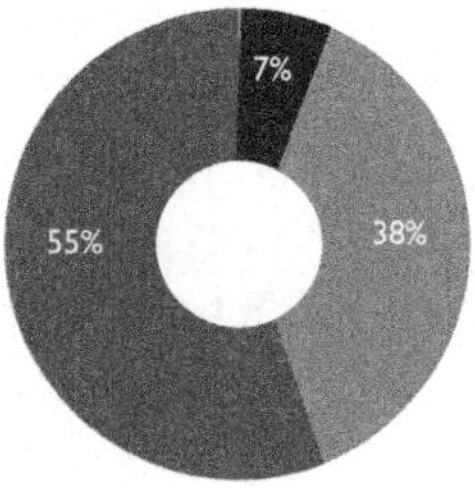

His research has been used ever since and is known as the 7/38/55 rule.

This rule breaks down to:

What you say	7% of meaning is communicated in the words people use
How you say it	38% of meaning is communicated in the tonality
Body language	55% of meaning is what the body language is saying

This is a useful rule to consider when we are communicating to one another. If 7% of the meaning of what the customer is saying is the words that they use, it can be easy to note that attentive listening, capturing all the facts of what the customer is telling you, could be a possible pitfall, as you could potentially miss 93% of the story.

Tonality

We have already spoken about tonal patterns in matching and mirroring, however, when actively listening to your customer, pay particular close attention to the inflection and variation in their voice. It will give you strong indicators of how they are expressing their feelings. If the volume goes up, it could demonstrate both excitement or frustration, and if it goes down, a more emotive state, which could be something painful or expressing some difficulty or dissatisfaction.

Tone is also about the variety and emphasis placed on certain aspects of the communication. You could pick up elements of sarcasm, some form of accusation, or warmth and pride.

What everybody is saying

A remarkable 55% of communication being received comes from body language. You need to look for congruence between what people say, how they say it and whether the body language is contradicting the words.

Be careful with this, it isn't the movies; if the body language is different to the words it does not mean they are lying! Take your time to watch what it is doing. Tapping the desk, bouncing the foot, rummaging through paperwork can all be signs of impatience, or nervousness or a feeling of being uncomfortable.

Reading body language is not about one thing, it is about combinations. You may have learnt that if someone has their arms crossed, they are demonstrating closed body language and defensive behaviour. Really? Do you know people who often sit with their arms crossed because it is comfortable to do so? In fact think back to school and/or university, there were plenty of teachers and lecturers that would walk round with their arms crossed. Not defensive, not closed, just comfortable.

Watch the eyes as an example. Bandler and Grinder first introduced the concept of eye movement patterns in their book *The Structure of Magic I: A Book About Language and Therapy*, which was published in 1975. In this book, they describe how they observed eye movements as a way of identifying the sensory modalities that people were using when thinking or recalling information, and how this could be used in therapy and communication. Utilising this can tell you what they are thinking and help you understand some of the meaning behind it. If they look up, for example, they tend to be picturing something in their mind, whereas when people engage with emotions, they have a strong tendency to glance downwards. These might be short flicks of the eye, but combine that with their tone, and the words, and you will get a much clearer picture of how they feel, and the meaning they have attributed to what they are saying.

Breathing is another thing to watch for – fast or shortness of breath vs deep breaths, or sighs and so on, give great insight into the emphasis of what is being discussed. Tony Robbins has spoken before about how matching breathing patterns can totally get you in sync with the other person and help you feel, how they feel.

It is not about you!

Consider what your mind is doing when it is listening to someone sharing their story or point of view. Interestingly, as it is listening it can be checking your own references to see if you have a similar viewpoint, experiences and thoughts. We are back to rapport again. The challenge when we are trying to do active listening is to switch this off, otherwise you will potentially miss what they are truly saying and therefore run the risk of using assumptive listening. In his 2003 book, Marshall Rosenberg describes four basic 'filters' or ways of interpreting communication that can interfere with clear understanding and connection: (1) judgements and evaluations, (2) comparisons, (3) demands, and (4) attributions of motive. He suggests that becoming aware of these filters and learning to communicate in a more empathic and compassionate way can help to create more meaningful and fulfilling relationships.

Don't blend the stories

The brain is a creative tool and will start to build images in your mind, and as someone shares with you their story the brain doesn't see that person in the story – it replaces them with you! Let's say someone is telling you about a time they went to Tanzania to climb Mount Kilimanjaro. They are explaining to you the trip, the various stages of the climb, from walking through the rainforest, across the desert known as the Saddle, and the final assent to the snow-covered summit, etc. In your mind, you are suddenly propelled to be the main character and it is you that is travelling up the mountain.

This is why you will hear people respond with quotes like 'wow, I can't believe you did that, I could never do that', or 'amazing, I would love that'. It's because their mind has taken them to the place and put them into the story. Or the frame of reference gets mixed with their own, and then they say 'let me tell you about the time I went ...'

Stop judging me

As the person starts to share with you the story, your brain listens, and you get this inner voice that starts talking to you; 'I wouldn't have done that, that's not how to do it, that's interesting, I know the answer to this, I've heard this before, this is to do with ...' In essence, you listen to the story and you are looking for answers.

Basically, the brain is in judgement mode, it is judging what they are telling you and trying to figure out the problem or solve the problem. This is a good thing, but while it is doing that, it is moving into a more social listening capacity, or the synapses of the brain keep flicking between listening and processing.

To truly listen, you need to turn off this inner voice, listen to the words, the tonality, and the body language, but how do you do that and how do you know when to then engage and speak?

Accessing the subconscious mind

A computer has some major parts, it has RAM where bits of data are held ready for immediate action, a hard disk, where it stores data, and then the processor which processes the information, and the type of processor determines how quickly it can do that.

Our brain processes and acts the same way. John Medina stated our brain runs on 12 watts of power and uses about 20% of the body's energy when it is in a rest state. Therefore, it is designed to run as efficiently as possible, almost in tick over, and will not fire up the brain unless it is necessary. Therefore, to truly get to understand your customer, and actively listen, you need to wait for the system to fire up, and then listen for the emotional aspects, as well as the thoughts of the customer.

Level 1 – Fast logic

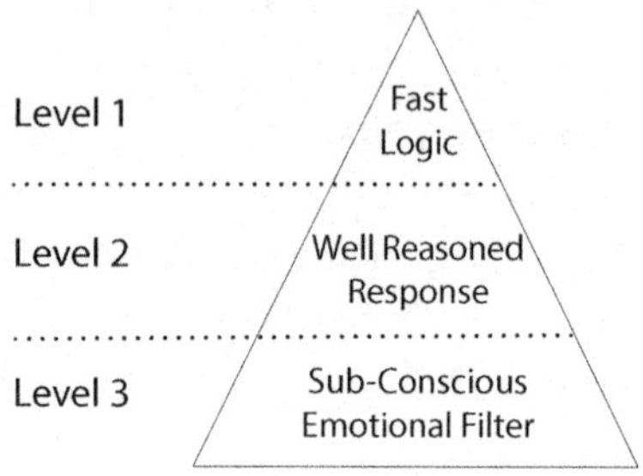

When the person you are talking to first starts to speak on a topic, they will give you information and data straight from RAM. The pieces of data held in short-term memory. This fast logic is interesting and will give you some background to the story and some form of context, but it doesn't provide many clues about the person, what they think or feel about the situation.

In psychology, this is sometimes referred to as noise as it can get in the way of understanding the real part of the story. Imagine you ask someone a simple question, 'how are you?' Quite often the response will be 'fine, thanks'. It is an instant response, and the computer doesn't want to fire up the processor and hard disk for this response. Even in a sales context, when you ask someone what they are looking for, they will provide you with some fast logic and tell you some top-line functionality or requirements.

Level 2 – Well-reasoned response

Once the person has shared with you the fast logic, and noticed that you are still interested and wanting more, the brain will need to fire up and add some processing power to the information, and potentially grab some more data from the memory banks. You will notice a change in the story at this point as the person either changes direction, moves to a different stance, or adds more colour to the story. Here you will get a lot more information, not only will you get a deeper context to the story but you may also get more subtext about the person's thinking and the meaning behind it.

Level 3 – Why the story is the story

The third level when listening is to understand why the story is the story.

The person won't say this, but you will be able to use your intuition and questions to try and establish and understand what is driving this person.

The subconscious level is where the drivers and emotions come from. It is the emotional filter that the person is using to drive the importance of this story or project that you are talking about.

To have the person share more and for you to be able to see beyond the facts and data, you will need to turn off your inner voice and seek more to understand. As the person is talking, you need to be thinking about why they are telling you this, why it is important to them, where this focus is coming from.

If you are going to ask questions, Steven Covey (*The 7 Habits of Highly Effective People*), suggests responding with a focus on how someone feels not on the facts. Replay them and wait for further information. 'You feel that ... can you tell me more?'

Finding the triggers

The whole idea of spotting emotional drivers sits by combining everything in this chapter. Utilise active listening and:

- listen to the words
- listen to the tonality
- spot the body language
- turn off that inner voice,
- ask yourself – 'Why are they telling me this, what is driving them, why is this important to them?'

These will enable you to spot either some of the eight types of drivers, but also hopefully more about the work-based drivers for this customer. Knowing what the work-based drivers are, will enable you to build into your initial engagement some triggers that will pique their interest, modify your sales presentations and value propositions to be more relatable to them, help shape conversations and build these people into champions, and overall build deeper more meaningful relationships where you are a trusted partner.

We look more at engaging the mind of your customer throughout the sales cycle in the second part of the book. Active listening is also looked at in this section where we look at engaging them emotionally through the use of questions and how to present solutions that will match directly to what the logical rational mind is thinking and also at a more emotional and subconscious level.

Part 2 – Salecology through the Sales Cycle

Understanding the various aspects of sales psychology is very useful and you saw in the Colourful Personalities chapter how to modify your sales approach to better engage and how to adapt your emails to gain better traction.

This part of the book takes a look at the various aspects of the sales cycle and how to modify your approach to better engage the customer in the sale and influence their mind, leading them to your products and services.

We have taken a usual buying cycle and sales process for this which includes:

Engagement	Connecting with customers and getting into a conversation
Explore	Influencing through questioning techniques that engage the brain
Demonstrate	How to lead the customer to your products and services and get them to see the benefits
Commit	How to overcome objections and negotiate the close.

The tools and techniques covered in this section are useful for all people who are involved in influencing outcomes, not just salespeople.

Let's talk

One of the challenges facing all sales roles is engaging customers into a conversation, either winning time to have the conversation or even getting the customer to respond to some form of outreach. The previous chapters, in Part 1 of the book, explain the different personality types and aspects which can turn people on or off you, but let us now take a dive into how to engage the customer in a conversation, and importantly how to ensure it is on a topic of your choice.

Do your research

Top salespeople do their homework; they know how important first impressions are and ensure they get it right by planning this part of the call. To do it right, they need plenty of data about the person to look for clues on how to engage them into the discussion.

Gaining insights

There are many tools available today to research your potential clients and understand their business, marketplace and more. You can look for news articles, what is happening in their industry, local environment, or the business challenges they are facing and so on. To be any value to the person you are calling, you don't just need to know about their business or industry, you will need an opinion on what is happening, why it's happening and how some people in similar situations are solving the puzzle. If you don't have this, why are you calling?

A quick acronym that you could use for this research is PESTEL. Introduced by Harvard Professor Francis J. Aguilar, in his 1967 book *Scanning the Business Environment,* a Pestel analysis enables you look at a company or industry across a multitude of factors and helps you gain a good overview of the marketplace, what things are affecting the business right now, wand hat is presenting opportunities and potential challenges.

P – Political	Brexit, tax policies, government stability, or change
E – Economical	Interest rates, inflation rates, economic stability
S – Social	Demographics, lifestyle and social factors like hybrid working

T – Technological	New technology, research and development, future shifts in tech
E – Environmental	Sustainability, environmental change, geographical location
L – Legislative	Employment law, labour law, health and safety

Utilise the acronym when conducting your research. Take each letter and consider what is happening in that area to get a strong understanding of the customer and 'put yourself in their shoes'. This will provide you in a strong position to engage with some background knowledge and an idea of why they should talk to you.

Once you are engaging with the customer you will need more information to be able to start to look for greater synergies and align your product and services to their business goals and objectives. So, it will also be worth looking on their website for any strategic objectives, current initiatives, company goals and aspirations, and news articles, etc.

Who are you calling?

The second part of your research is to determine who to call, and in terms of a business-to-business sale, their role and function in the organisation. You will often have a variety of people you can target across an organisation and the key is to determine whether the person has influence or authority to enable a decision to be taken by the organisation to buy your products or services. Robert Miller and Stephen Heiman in 1985 published their book on strategic selling which was one of the first introductions to different types of buyers within businesses. They described them as Economic Buyers, Technical Buyers and User Buyers, a concept that has stuck over the past few decades.

In essence, you can break down different types of buyers and stakeholders in the organisation as follows:

- Strategic
- Managerial
- Operational

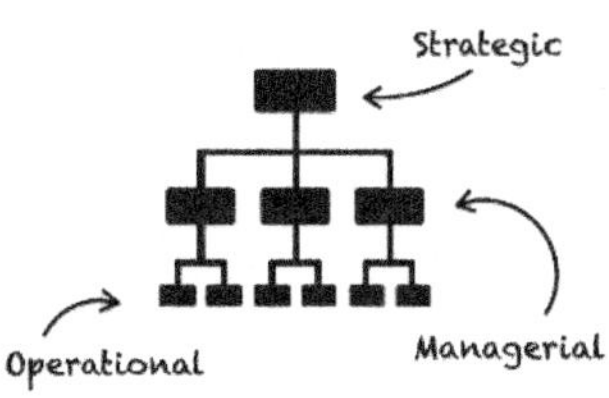

Strategic buyers

The strategic-level contact is ultimately in charge of the department and the person who holds the purse strings. Often referred to as the Economic

Buyer, they are usually one of the most senior people, although not always, and will often be focused on return on investment and evidence that you can deliver tangible benefit to their business, i.e. will it help deliver the company goals, reduce cost, speed up processes, enable the business to grow, etc. This level of contact will also be keen to evaluate the risk of purchasing your solution.

When dealing with a strategic-level contact you must consider their business strategy and how your product or service will support them in achieving their long-term objectives.

Managerial buyers

The managerial-level contact is someone (can be more than one) who is often running the day-to-day operations of the department and will be interested in the technical aspects of the solution such as functionality, process and infrastructure. The manager will be focused on evaluating the feasibility of the proposed solution and will be interested in whether the product or service will work for their team.

They will be interested in the technical aspects of your product and service so are often termed as the Technical Buyers. During your proposal and any demonstration, they will watch with particular interest and will be looking for how it will impact their business, check for any compliance issues, system integration challenges, and how it will ultimately be utilised. You must consider how they will adopt your product and services into their operations and deliver impact.

Operational buyers

The operational level of contact will be linked personally to your solution and judge it based on the impact it will have on their specific job performance. They will be evaluating how the product or service will be used on a daily basis and whether it will have a positive impact.

Warning!

Be careful not to spend too much time talking to people who are not in a position to influence a decision or give you access to key stakeholders, i.e. operational level. That is not to say don't talk to them, they can be great coaches and provide us with the information you need to follow up on, however, just remember your time is limited and use it sparingly. Some training will tell you to get as high up the organisation chart as you can, as early as you can. Take that advice with a quick reality check. If the company you are calling is a small-to-medium-size business that might work, however, if you are calling a larger organisation, and get in touch with a senior leader, they will not have time for someone who cannot add value straight away. You don't know their business and you don't know their organisational needs, so what do you want from them – to start asking some questions? If they take your call, and potentially engage a little, they will quickly push you back down the org chart to someone else – 'you should speak to …' – and potentially will be tough to re-engage. You would have been better off working at technical level and then engaging once you have established some real needs and could then present those in the first meeting with the strategic buyer.

Knowing which level of person you are going to be contacting will enable you to adjust your communication level accordingly.

The three whys

Having completed your research and figured out who you want to contact, before diving into making the call you will need to be able to answer these three simple, but very effective, qualification questions:

Why change	Why should the customer change from what they already have or are already doing?
Why now	Why should they do it now and not put it off for next month, next quarter, next year?
Why us	Why should they choose you and your business to buy from?

When you are considering calling a new prospect or opportunity, or about to introduce a new concept or idea to an existent client, you should have a hypothesis that can answer these three questions. If you don't have a thought about why they should change, then why are you calling? I first came across these in Neil Rackham's 1988 book on spin selling, where he emphasises the importance of asking these questions in order to understand the customer's buying process and to create more effective sales strategies.

The answers to these three questions provide essential top-line qualification on every opportunity in your pipeline. If you are unable to answer these three questions with certainty, the chances are it is not a good deal to be forecasting. Hence, the three whys give you wisdom of what to and what not to put in your forecast. They will also give you direction on where you are weak in the sale and what you need to focus on to move the business forward.

Why change?

This relates to changes the customer is experiencing. What change has happened that has or could stimulate them entering a buying process? What pain have you identified that the customer is experiencing or will be experiencing in the future? How big are or will the pains be? What impact is it having on the business and the individuals inside? What metrics could you associate to the pain? Is the change industrywide or just localised to your customer? Your PESTEL analysis can give provide you with the why change.

Why now?

This relates to the customer's awareness of the need to do something based on the changes that are going on. Obviously during the conversation, you will need to uncover how big the pain is, and what is the win for the customer if they are solved. What metrics can you identify either externally for now, to show the customer what others are doing and therefore the likely return on investment they will gain by addressing them now? What impact will they avoid and is it sufficiently compelling to act now? Depending on your research and analysis, you may have also identified some compelling events, such as legislation changes, that might force the customer to act now. If not FOMO – fear of missing out – can also be used, i.e. the opportunity cost of not doing it now.

Why us?

What is it that you will provide the customer that gives you some form of competitive advantage? Why will the customer want to use us as opposed to:

- solving the problem internally
- choosing another supplier
- staying with the incumbent/do nothing?

Consider what your products and services can offer to resolve the problems and how you can differentiate them from others, but also remember people buy from people they trust. As you get into the conversation you can obviously lead the customer to your solutions but for the first part of engaging you need to ensure your hypothesis starts to match why they should talk to you.

Three whys warning!

At the beginning of a sales process, the three whys will typically be in your voice and words. You will create a hypothesis based on why you believe the customer might want to change (this may be related to circumstances being faced by other companies in that sector or insight and intelligence gained from previous conversations, your network or reading something in the press), why they would do it now and why they would want to do it with you and your company (this will typically be relevant metrics or case studies from similar customers).

However, as the customer's buying process progresses, the answer to the three whys will need to be in the customer's voice and words. This is because if the customer cannot answer the three whys for themselves, they won't be able to sell it internally to others; or later in the sales process, normally right before taking the decision to buy, they will ask themselves these three questions in some sort of fashion. Questions like: 'why don't we simply stick to what we have' or 'can't we save the money and put this off to another time' or, 'the current supplier has offered us a better rate not to cancel, maybe we should stay with them'. To help negate the effects of self-deception and being overly optimistic that the customer will go ahead, when answering the three whys as you go through the sales process, qualify what you believe to be true by using the phrase 'they have told me'!

Opening the call

Having completed your research, and considered the three whys, it's time to plan to make the call. Opening a call for the first time is quite different from being in a meeting room or having several people on a call later in the sales cycle.

The saying goes that first impressions are made within the first 30 seconds of meeting someone. This may be true for face-to-face meetings, but over the phone you may only have a few seconds to grab the prospect's interest otherwise they will hang up.

From experience, you have two initial phases to hook the customer into a conversation with you:

- the first 10 seconds – so they don't hang up on a sales call; and
- the next 20 seconds to engage them into dialogue.

Elevator pitch – it's a bit old skool!

You may have been taught to craft an elevator pitch. The term is often attributed to Ilene Rosenzweig and Michael Caruso, who were both executives at *Vanity Fair* magazine in the 1990s. According to some accounts, the term was coined during a conversation between Rosenzweig and Caruso, who were discussing how to pitch ideas to their boss during a brief elevator ride. The term 'elevator pitch' gained popularity in the early 2000s as a way to describe a concise and persuasive sales pitch that can be delivered in the time it takes to ride an elevator.

To be fair, elevator pitches are useful for that moment when you are at a dinner engagement, or having drinks with a customer and someone else in the group says, 'oh what do you do? '. Then maybe it is a great time for a short 30 to 60 sec intro into your world. But on the phone, or in a meeting, it is too salesy in today's world to lead with an elevator pitch. For many years, opening statements have been the go-to way of opening a meeting or a sales call or an email. Develop some hooks to grab their attention and hopefully they will engage. Well, yes, these do work, but you need to amend the way you build these to grab the customer's attention and remove the fight-or-flight response.

Part of the challenge today is that our customers are double busy. When they receive your email, sales call or even when they have a meeting booked with you, when the meeting kicks off, the customer's mind is busy elsewhere, worrying about the previous meeting or different fires they are trying to put out. Your opening statement, or as we call it, your initial positioning statement, needs to grab their attention, engage their left and right brain, and snap them into paying attention to you.

Initial positioning statements

An initial positioning statement (IPS) is a statement made by the caller giving the customer a sound reason for your contact, telling them why they should talk to you in terms of the value you can provide. It should answer 'what's in it for the customer'. In essence, there are three golden rules for an IPS:

1. It's about the customer not the seller
2. It is tailored to the customer
3. It includes a teach

Who is this call for – you or them?

In order for an IPS to work it needs to be about the customer, not about you or your company. If you listen to the way many salespeople try to open the call it is about trying to provide reasons about why the seller wants the call, but not about why the customer should be interested.

Words like the following are about you, not the customer:

I am just calling to find out how you …
I am calling to introduce …
I just wanted to know how you …'

Even when people try to make it about 'what's in it for the customer', they still end up making it about themselves. Here is a typical example from an organisation that already supplies to one part of the business and is trying to gain access to another:

Seller	*Hi is that Lee?*
Cust	*Yes*
Seller	*It's Darren calling from Links Inc, how you doing today?*
Cust	*Great, busy, what's up?*
Seller	*I wanted to give you a quick call to introduce myself, I work with Sandy over in your central production plant, and I wanted to drop you a call and introduce myself, share with you some of the great work we are doing for them, and find out more about your plant and see if there are any mutual opportunities for us to work together on?*

You can see from the dialogue that the seller is trying to show what's in it for the customer but it is still all about the seller, I want, I would like, I thought. In the recipient's mind what they hear is, I work with Steve and sell them stuff and want to speak to you to see if I can sell you some stuff.

Teach and tailored

The IPS will need to include how will it help the client and be focused on a problem or a need and provide a solid business reason for the sales call or meeting. It helps answer the why change.

One of the challenges in grabbing the customer's attention is to get them to listen in the first instance and secondly demonstrating to them that you are someone worth talking to. During the recession in 2011, Brent Adamson and Matthew Dixon et al conducted some interesting research on how to make sells when the market is depressed. In their book, *The Challenger Sale*, they introduced the idea of Teaching for Differentiation and Tailoring for Resonance. Taking this concept and bringing it into an IPS, you must teach the customer something quickly to raise their interest and engage them into a conversion. This will engage both their left and right brain and hopefully snap them into listening and engaging.

By tailoring the teach to be around their industry, about other people in similar roles, and how they have overcome similar challenges, will resonate strongly with the prospect and will help demonstrate your credibility and why they would benefit from talking to you.

Delivering the teach in an IPS

To build a great IPS that includes a teach and is tailored to the customer, consider the following format after initial introductions:

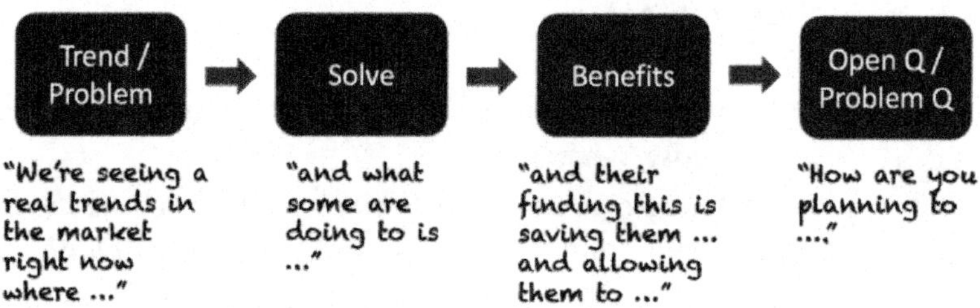

1: Start with a trend or problem

By starting off your IPS by sharing an understanding of a trend or a problem you are observing in the marketplace will immediately begin to establish some rapport and credibility with the customer. This should come from your research and insight conducted previously. Again, make sure that it is tailored to resonate.

On its own this is not enough to get the customer talking because it hasn't taught them anything apart from you are familiar with the issue or problem. Utilise your research here to ensure you are hot on current issues or trends. Use phrases like:

We are seeing a real trend in the market right now where …

I have been speaking to a lot of (enter job title here) who are sharing with us that …

This probably sounds familiar and what many people already do as part of the opening statement. However, what usually happens is that then they either talk about what their company is doing and why they have built a new product, or they go straight to the question, 'are you seeing that?', it is too early for pitching, and too early to ask questions. The customer is still on alert and not ready to engage.

2: Tell them what other people in their position are doing to resolve it
Giving them the second part of the statement demonstrates to the customer that you know the answer to the problem. It is really important here that you establish yourself as a credible person, so the solution is not 'by using our product', it is more how they are fixing it, rather than what they are fixing it with. This will ensure your IPS isn't sales lead, more teaching led.

By making it about what others are doing also makes the story more plausible. People tend to believe stories told about other people rather than the storyteller themselves.

We are seeing a real trend in the market right now where…

and what some (insert similar job title here) are doing to mitigate this is …

The customer is clever enough to understand the reason you are sharing the story is because you are part of the solution so there is no requirement for you to talk about your company or product. That said, you will also need to finish with the benefits of the story to show the customer the impact it has.

3: Share the benefits they are receiving
The final part of the IPS is to show the benefits they are experiencing now they have fixed the problem. This third part of the statement links left and right sides of the brain and builds an emotive reason to engage now into the conversion.

We are seeing a real trend in the market right now where …

What some (insert similar job title here) are doing to mitigate this is …

and what they are finding is that it is saving them … and allowing them to …

4: Ask a problem-based question

To engage the customer in the conversation, you must invite them through a well-timed and placed question, which should be linked to the problem, and preferably not a generic open-ended question.

We are seeing a real trend in the market right now where …

What some (insert similar job title here) are doing to mitigate this is …

And what they are finding now is that it is saving them … and allowing them to …

is that something you are seeing in your organisation?

Using a problem question should engage the customer to instantly start to agree or disagree with the example provided and will allow you to continue in the discussion.

The IPS is designed solely to get the customer to engage into a conversation on a topic of your choice. Your research and positioning will be key in crafting a well-targeted IPS that resonates with the prospect and already will start to lead the customer towards your products and services.

Coming back to our Salecology colour personalities, these IPSs work with all four colours.

- Red – it cuts to the point and shows me the benefits of the conversation
- Blues – you are giving me detail and I will be interested to hear more
- Greens – the story is about others, and therefore you are showing me you care
- Oranges – it involves storytelling and invites them to speak, so they will enjoy both.

Also an IPS can be modified to be used in emails, potentially with some bullet points, face-to-face meetings to kick off the conversation, and also as an opening for a telephone call.

Lead the customer to the solution

As we discussed at the beginning of this book, the late 70s saw sales migrate from that bring and brag, spray and pray approach into the solution-based sales era. Since then, the cornerstone of all great salespeople has been to ask great questions, but why do we ask questions? The truth be told, any salesperson worth their salt already knows the typical problems their customer will have, and they also know what they need to do to fix it! If only the customer would simply give them the cash – they could implement their product or service and solve the problems instantly and deliver some amazing benefits.

Out of the tens of thousands of salespeople we have coached around the globe, when asked the question 'why do we ask questions?', the universal response is to find out the pain or problems of the customer, or find out where they are coming from, so we can tailor our solution to meet their needs. On the face of it, this intuitive response makes perfect sense but those that are focused on this are really missing the bigger opportunities and are failing to influence the customer.

In Stephen Covey's bestseller, *7 Habits of Highly Effective People*, his fifth habit is 'Seek first to understand – and then be understood'. This is often misinterpreted to mean ask questions and then share your opinion. In reality, he is talking about 'The Habit of Mutual Understanding'. He is talking about understanding each other and working together – not questioning techniques.

The typical mistake that some salespeople make is asking some basic background questions, not listening to the response, and then diving into selling features and benefits of their product or service. We discussed in the chapter 'There is no such thing as a no brainer' that we need to engage the customer's intellectual brain, and also their emotional irrational brain.

Leading with the solution

Asking these foundational questions and diving into features and benefits doesn't really influence the mind, we need to lead the customer to the solution rather than lead with it. The first problem occurs by the lack of information gathered during the questions. The salesperson asks some questions to understand the customer's needs or some background questions to understand what they are looking for. Using a TV sales as an example:

What TV do you have at the moment?

What size are you looking for?

What do you like to watch on the TV, is it sports, movies?

These are fair questions and start to help the salesperson narrow down the options and products they want to show the customer. The salesperson will take that data they uncovered and move to the product and try to pitch one or a small variety of TVs, showing some of the features they have and why, in the salesperson's opinion, one is better than the other. The customer will listen to what they have to say, judge the sales demonstration, determine whether they like it, don't like it and so on. This could end with a sale – sounds good! – or with one of two types of objections:

- Price objection
- General objection

Price objections

Price objections occur if the product has far too many features, i.e. a lot more than the customer is really looking for, and because of that they feel that they don't want to pay for things they don't want or need. You will hear statements like 'it seems a bit complicated' or 'it's a lot more than we are looking for'; you may also hear questions like 'do you have a lesser model or a cheaper option?' or 'can you take some of those features off, then how much will it cost?'.

A TV sale these days is becoming more of a commodity item and it is getting harder to differentiate why the price variation can be $2,000 between TV sets of the same size. This is even more exemplified in the software as a service market, where the salesperson wants to show all the things the software can do. The customer can be overwhelmed by the service and find that it does a lot more than they need and, therefore, it seems rather complicated. Even *if* they may gain some benefit from it in the long run, they can't see the need for it now and therefore won't want to pay for it now.

General objections

Salespeople have also been taught to sell the benefits of the features by explaining the 'so what?'. In general terms the 'so what' is how the feature can help the customer. Taking the TV example above, it would sound something like:

Feature:	*The TV comes with five pre-set viewing modes based on the type of TV viewing you are watching,*
So what:	*which means that when you watch movies or sports, you can change the mode to get a much better definition and picture.*

This is more influential as you are showing the customer how it could help, unfortunately the customer still sits and listens to your pitch to determine if it is worth having or paying for. It then leads to a more general objection, 'I can see why some people want that, but it's not really what I am looking for!'

Leading with the solution therefore will ultimately end with you back in the history books of 'spray and pray'. It is in the hope that if you tell the customer enough about the product, they will like what you say and buy it. Of course, it does sometimes work, especially if the customer has already decided to buy. Unfortunately, it won't allow you to upsell or cross sell to different products and services, and to be honest, you haven't influenced the customer's mind, you have simply taken the order. Leading with the solution, therefore, has little influence on the customer's mind, they sit in judgement on your sales pitch, make up their own mind if it is of benefit to them, and which parts they like or dislike.

The best way to lead the customer to the solution is to truly understand what problems your features solve and build some of your questions to uncover those problems.

Fabs to riches

One of my long-term frustrations is that the sales team are taught their products either by a product development team or by marketing. Marketing, being a broadcast medium, talk about how they feel people could benefit from the product. This is very generalised because they are talking about how it might help anyone. They call this features and benefits. In sales we have a one-to-one relationship with our customer so we don't need to talk in general, we can ask our customers questions and talk specifically about their needs. Not all features will be needed by the customer, no matter how helpful they are, they are just advantages of the product, but not of benefit to that specific customer. Hence, we talk about features, advantages and benefits.

In truth the concept of features, advantages and benefits (FAB) was first introduced by Theodore Levitt, a marketing professor at Harvard Business School, in the 1960s. He developed the FAB framework to help companies improve their marketing and sales messaging by focusing on the value that a product or service offers to customers.

However, in his framework he was using advantages as a competitive advantage or the positive aspects of the features that make the product or service better than alternatives.

Tom Hopkins modified advantages in his 1980 book *How to Master the Art of Selling*, in which he broke down the features of the product or service into advantages, which are the positive aspects of those features, and then into benefits, which are the specific ways in which the product or service will improve the customer's life or solve a problem. By presenting the benefits in a clear and compelling way, salespeople can help potential customers understand why the product or service is worth buying, and overcome objections based on cost or other factors. Here is a quick breakdown for you.

Features

Features are characteristics of your product or service. It is what the product has or does and they are easy to talk about, for example features of an iPhone are the super high-quality camera, iMessage, Facetime and the iOS operating system. Features are not only linked to products, for example your organisations may be more service-led so it could be features such as lead times, your innovation team, the depth of coverage and so on. Everything that you sell will have some sort of features.

In all the research we have read, there is little evidence that links salespeople talking about features to sales conversion.

Selling on features lead to price objections

One of the glitches a lot of salespeople make is 'feature dumping'. They seem to believe that if they continue to tell the customer a list of features, they will be impressed and will be interested. The real answer is quite the opposite. As we discussed on the previous pages, when a customer hears a long list of features, they tend to consider the product is too complicated, or it does a lot more than they need, and therefore ask for a discount, ask for things to be taken off, or ask for a lesser/cheaper model.

Advantages

Advantages are how the product can help – anyone. As said early, this is how the features can help people in general. Advantage statements typically come in the format of 'because of (insert feature) you can do (insert advantage)'. They are more persuasive than features, especially in the beginning of the sales cycle, but as the sales cycle progresses, advantage statements have a reduced impact on influencing the customer. Customers might be interested to hear how others have used the product, and how it has helped them, but very quickly they are more interested in how it might meet their own requirements.

The marketing materials you have at your disposal will call them benefits but they are really advantages because they are generic and not tailored to each specific prospect or customer.

Selling on advantages leads to general objections

Don't be fooled with advantage statements that talk about saving time and money, surely everyone wants to save time and money, right? Wrong! Not everyone is motivated by saving time and money, I am sure you have heard people say – 'it doesn't matter how much it costs, as long as it fixes the problem.' Also, everyone is selling time and money savings these days. I think it is more advantageous to ask what they would do with the time – that might be more beneficial. Below is an example of how advantages lead to an objection (utilising the iPhone as an example)

Salesperson: *Having iMessage on your phone means you can send messages using the data network and not pay for picture messages.*

Customer: *I can see why some people can use that, but my friends have Android handsets and iMessages can't send to those, so it's not that useful to me.*

Benefits

As we have now established, benefits are how a product or service meets the customer's expressed needs. Demonstrating benefits are the most influential and powerful behaviour a salesperson can exhibit.
Benefit statements can only be made once you understand the customer's needs and the value associated with meeting these needs. In essence, if the customer hasn't said they want or need it, it ceases to be a benefit.

USPs or DSPs

Selling used to be about sharing with customers your USPs, your unique selling points, but as the world becomes smaller, and speed of product development increases, it is becoming tougher to differentiate products and create things that are truly unique. Added on to that, the internet has made customers believe that whatever you are selling they can probably buy somewhere else and probably cheaper, whether this is true or not. Features however, do not have to be USPs, they can also be DSPs, distinctive selling points.

Unique selling point (USP)	What your product or company does differently that makes it unique
Distinctive selling point (DSP)	Things your product or company does better than others

Distinctive selling points are aspects that your company, product or collection of features can do better than the competition. Taking the mobile phone again as an example, when the iPhone launched it most definitely wasn't the best phone on the market; it wasn't first to have a touchscreen, it wasn't first to play music and it wasn't the first to be able to browse the internet and it wasn't first to package it altogether in one unit. The market leader at that time was Nokia, who brought out the Nokia N95 to stop Apple in its tracks. Designed to be the most powerful phone on the market, cheaper than the new market entry from Apple, and designed to have all the latest features plus more. But Apple made its product more distinctive. It looked different to everyone else, they advertised it differently to everyone else, and homed in on making it cool and fashionable rather than all about technical specifications and features.

Why ask questions?

Coming back to the beginning of this chapter, we were talking about why ask questions and how to lead customers to the solution, rather than with it. To do this it starts with product knowledge and understanding what problems your features solve. If you know what problems your features solve you can ask the customer about those issues and lead them towards your product.

The best way to figure out what questions to ask is to reverse the advantages statements to understand the problems the features solve. Below are three features of an iPhone and the advantages of those features. Remember – they are not benefits if the customer doesn't want or need them!

Feature	Advantage
Streams music	Listen to music on the go No need to download music Access to millions of tracks
48mpx camera	Professional photos every time Saves carrying multiple devices Don't miss out on those memories
iCloud	Backs up your phone in case you lose it Shares photos, contacts, calendar across all your devices Frees up memory on your phone so it runs faster

To lead the customer to the solutions we need to uncover whether the customer has a need for any of these advantages, so by thinking about what problems a customer may have that these could solve we can get to the questions.

Pain and gain analysis

Many different books utilise the idea of pain and gain, especially when selling solutions, indeed Michael Bosworth's *Solution Selling* book discusses in depth what he calls the Pain Chain. Below is a good way to think through your offerings and consider the answer to it. We have used the phrase 'pain and gain analysis'. The left-hand side looks at the pain customers could have, and the right-hand side the gain they would have if they had the feature.

Let's take a different feature for the iPhone this time – Siri, the voice-activated companion that can do many things for you on the iPhone.

Pain		**Gain**	
What problem our feature solves	**What are the consequences of the problem**	**What do they need to fix the problem**	**What benefits could they gain from it**
• Messaging when driving	• Put lives at risk • Fined if caught • Lose licence	• Ability to listen and answer texts without touching my phone	• Keep everyone safe • Utilise my time more effectively • Get back to people quickly

You could spend quite a while listing lots of problems the feature can fix. Learning your products and services this way will enable you to lead the customer to your solution so much easier and tailor an offering that is just right for them.

To finish off, below is an example of questions that lead the customer to the solution:

Seller — *Are you worried about using your phone when driving?*

Customer — *Yes, I often get a lot of text messages while I am driving, and I worry about not getting back to the customers quick enough – to be honest I do check them sometimes while I am driving.*

Seller — *Naughty, what will happen if you get caught?*

Customer — *I know, the fines are pretty hefty, and I certainly can't afford to lose my licence, I have to drive for work.*

Seller — *So if you could simply ask your phone to read the text to you, would that make a difference?'*

Customer — *Really, can it do that? That would be cool, it would of course keep me safer, and stop me running the risk of being fined by the police.'*

Seller — *And getting back to your customers instantly, would that help maintain your sales?*

Customer — *Definitely, my customers' expect a very quick reply and turnaround, that's why we use messaging instead of email.*

Benefit statement – Well that's exactly what Siri can do for you, you simply ask Siri to read your messages and they will be read out loud to you, and then Siri will ask you if you would like to respond. You simply speak your message and it will be converted into text and sent back.

This example shows how to lead the customer to the feature not with it. The customer now sees value in and has taught the salesperson what they need to demonstrate on the product in order to win the sale.

In the next chapter you will find different types of questions that also influence the customer's mind, and how to get them further engaged in your products and services.

Which is more important – pain or gain?

One of the interesting psychological factors often overlooked by sales and marketeers is how much weight is placed on the fear of loss versus the power of gain. Many people want to tell you about the features and benefits of the product, how it helps, how you will benefit from having it and so on. This doesn't always tempt people into buying.

In 1979, psychologists Daniel Kahneman and Amos Tversky, published an academic paper which discussed 'loss aversion' as part of their research on decision making under uncertainty. This paper, and subsequent research into cognitive bias, helped Kahneman go on to receive a Nobel Prize in economics. They found that people typically experience about twice as much psychological pain from a loss as they do pleasure from an equivalent gain. For example, losing $100 may be more painful than the pleasure received of winning $100. People are more motivated to avoid losses than they are to pursue gains.

This bias can have a significant impact on decision making in various areas of life, including financial decisions, gambling and even interpersonal relationships. Understanding loss aversion is crucial for salespeople who want to create effective marketing and sales strategies and drive revenue for their business.

FOMO

Sales and marketing have used a type of loss aversion to their advantage by emphasising the potential losses that customers could incur if they don't purchase a product or service. By framing the benefits of a product or service in terms of what the customer stands to lose if they don't buy it, salespeople can tap into the customer's fear of missing out (FOMO) and create a sense of urgency to act.

One of the most common ways you will see this used is by creating a sense of scarcity around a product or service. This can be done by emphasising that the product or service is only available for a limited time, or that there are only a limited number of units available, or limited-edition versions. Thus, creating a fear of missing out and generating a sense of urgency to motivate the customer to take action before it is too late.

Another example of FOMO when selling a training programme might be to emphasise that the programme is designed to help customers advance their career and that those who don't take advantage of it could miss out on valuable career opportunities.

Financial losses are also another way to consider FOMO by emphasising the potential losses that a customer could incur if they don't go ahead and take the decision sooner rather than later.

Loss aversion – can stop people buying

Loss aversion is more than the fear of missing out on the new shiny product or financial opportunities. People may be reluctant to try new products because they fear the potential losses that could result from making a bad purchase, or sometimes that residual satisfaction they have with their existing products and services. Understanding how loss aversion affects buying behaviour can help you develop strategies to overcome this bias and encourage consumers to try and buy new products. According to Dan Ariely (*Predictably Irrational*) there are lots of reasons why loss aversion can stop people from buying. These include:

- Status quo bias
- Residual satisfaction

- Cost
- Time of learning something new
- What if I make the wrong choice
- FOMO – on a better option

One of the key reasons that loss aversion stops people from buying new products is that people are often more aware of the potential losses associated with a new purchase than they are of the potential gains. When people are considering buying a new product, they may focus on the features and benefits of the product, but they may also worry about potential downsides, such as the risk of wasting money on something that doesn't work as expected. This uncertainty will then lead them to question whether they really want or need it, or should stick with what they already have.

When people are faced with a decision, they often default to the option that feels most familiar, even if it may not be the best option available. This bias can be especially strong when it comes to buying new products because people may be reluctant to take a risk on something that they are not familiar with – hence they tend to renew existing contracts, buy the same car (only newer), and so on. When people have been using a particular product for a long time, they may be reluctant to switch to a new product because they are comfortable with the old one and may not want to learn how to use a new product. This can be especially true for products that are complex or that require a significant investment of time to learn how to use effectively.

We spoke about the fear of missing out to create the reason to change but people may be reluctant to try a new product because they fear that they will miss out on something better if they make the wrong choice. You see this when people like something but still feel they want to shop around before going ahead and buying it. This fear can be especially strong in situations where there are many similar products on the market, and it can make it difficult for consumers to take a decision on selecting one.

How to utilise loss aversion

So, how can you overcome loss aversion and encourage consumers to try new products? One strategy is to offer consumers a risk-free trial of the new product. This can help to overcome the practical concerns that can contribute to loss aversion by giving consumers the opportunity to try the product before committing to a purchase. By offering a risk-free trial, businesses can help to overcome the cost and difficulty of switching from one product to another, as well as the fear of missing out on something better.

Free trails, test drives and extended trials, have been used for decades and are also known as the 'puppy dog close'. Giving something to someone and then taking it away, also creates the sense of loss, or invokes the loss aversion – i.e. I don't want to give it back.

You can also encourage consumers to try new products by offering incentives or rewards for doing so. For example, businesses could offer discounts or other incentives to customers who try a new product and provide feedback on their experience.

In bigger, more considered sales you get more time to engage and ask deeper questions. Understanding that the person will be more motivated, especially initially, with the sense of loss, you must spend time upfront to build and influence the 'why change'.

In *Think Fast and Slow*, Daniel Kahneman discusses status quo bias on how people make decisions. Everything in the previous paragraphs indicates the status quo bias will take precedent if you do not uncover and build, in their mind, the need to change. What are they losing because of the problems that they are currently experiencing. The temptation will be to consider the money they could be getting, or the benefits they could be having, this isn't a psychological loss, this is a gain!

You must spend time understanding what has changed and how that is now affecting them. This may not have been the case when they bought their previous product or service, it solved some of the problems they were experiencing at the time, but what is now happening that is causing them some serious issues and is creating the loss. Are they wasting time, losing money, projects are being held back, bottlenecks are causing process or workflow issues, strategies and plans are being stifled, and so on? This will have more of an immediate, emotional engagement as they have a stronger initial cognitive bias than how much more they could be gaining.

For those selling into organisations, these cognitive biases also sit in the different stakeholders of the business. The CEO, CFO, VPs and all the other stakeholders have a stronger link to loss aversion when it comes to decision making and taking. Overall, understanding loss aversion and using it effectively in sales strategies can help you increase conversion rates and ultimately drive more revenue for the business.

Influence the mind through questions

Questions form part of rapport building. Neuroscience has shown the human mind enjoys being stimulated and if someone is asking us questions, showing a genuine interest, then it helps build a connection between us. Don't make the common mistake of thinking that people love talking about themselves! This is a fallacy. Do you like talking about yourself? Most people find talking about themselves embarrassing. What people like talking about are topics they are interested in; yes, they may share a story about a time they did this or that, but it's about the story, not themselves in particular.

The real power in questions is to engage the customer into the conversation, spark their conscious mind and awaken their emotions. You want to move them into an 'inquisitive' mindset and lead them towards your products and services. Questions can be used to prime the customer's mind, influence their thinking, and influence them into shaping a potential solution. Through the use of questions, the skilful consultant can plant ideas and have the customer build a solution that just so happens to match their products and services.

Open or closed questions?

Sales 101 focuses on teaching people how to use OPEN and CLOSED questions. You learn that open questions 'open the customer up' and are used to gain information, and closed questions are used to 'close the customers down' and are used to confirm information.

OPEN questions – who, what, where, when, why, how?

CLOSED questions – do, are, is, could, would, can?

As much as everyone is taught these question types there has been no evidence over the past 50 years that demonstrates that those who ask open or closed questions or a combination of each are more successful than others. The original research started in the 70s by Neil Rackham, author of *Spin Selling*, analysed an initial 6,000 sales calls, and couldn't make the link between open and closed questions and success.

The answer to these types of questions will be totally distorted because of human nature. The inflection in your voice, your pace, pitch, tone and volume will all have an impact on what the other person hears. We discussed previously the power of rapport. If you are in rapport, the other person is already finishing off your sentences before you even get to it. They intuitively know that even if you ask a closed question you might be actually asking a wider question. If you are asked the question in a classroom, 'do you know the difference between open and closed questions?', your brain connects the dots and you would ascertain that you are being asking to share or explain to me the difference – not just say 'Yes' and walk off. It's the same question when you are in a restaurant and the waiter comes over and says 'Can I get you some drinks?'. You wouldn't just say yes and leave it at that.

Let's take a look at some other question types that are useful.

Reflective questions

Reflective questions are used to reflect back the last part of an answer to create your next question. They are excellent questions for building conversations without you having to think of the next 'killer' question.

Equally these are also useful when customers use terminology and assume you know what they mean by it. If they then assume you know – this could lead you to making some big mistakes.

Customer: *Not knowing when to call the customer is a real nightmare for me.*
Seller: *When you say nightmare, what do you mean exactly?*

Customer: *I'm looking for something modern.*
Seller: *Modern means a lot of different things to different people, when you say modern, what does that look like to you?*

Leading/probing questions

These questions are used to lead the customer in the direction you want and probe them further to get better clarity and understanding.

Leading questions are deliberately designed to make the other person think in a certain way. They usually include the answer or point the customer in the right direction. When used skilfully, you can plant the answers in the customer's mind and get better answers. For example:

How quickly did you need this implemented – implies that they are going ahead

Subtle probing questioning can also be loaded with some leading words that plant ideas into customers' minds. Take a look at these two questions. Changing one word leads the customer to demonstrate the problem is bigger:

Does that problem happen frequently, and if so, how often?
Does that problem happen occasionally, and if so, how often?

Eric Loftus conducted research on the use of wording which found that this subtle type of change can demonstrate a 300% increase in how often that problem occurred.

Direct questions

These help to clarify information or challenge the customer when you ask a straight-to-the-point question. Too many times, a seller asks a direct question, hears silence coming back and then fills that vacuum with their own voice again.

Seller: *If your existing provider came back with a better price, would you still want to move away from them?*
(Customer is silent as they think about the answer. They are just about to say 'yes' when the salesperson butts in.)

Seller: We're happy to work alongside them, if that's what you want to do?
(The seller has let the customer off the hook from making a commitment!)

TED questions

TED questions are very helpful questions. TED stands for:

- Tell me
- Explain to me
- Describe to me.

These are excellent questions for gaining a lot of information from one question.

Tell me John, what is really important to you regarding this project?
Can you describe to me your organisational structure?
Could you explain to me how this problem is affecting your business right now?

There are two things at play in TED questions. Firstly, there is an implied command in the use of these words, it's as if you are giving the customer an order. Secondly, these types of words can take people back to their childhood where their parents would use similar words, especially when used with their first name. It subconsciously raises the seller's authority in the customer's eyes. Think about your doctor, they use TED questions not only to root out the data they need to diagnose the problem but also to present themselves as an authority figure.

TED questions are also very good at bringing a customer back on topic especially if they have gone off on a tangent.

Hypothetical questions

Hypothetical questions are great for projecting the customer forward in their thought processes. You can move them into a mindset that gets them to consider the question 'What if …?'. It can be used to help them consider potential problems or consequences should something happen, or they can be used to consider potential upsides should they have the advantages of your product or service.

Customer: *This issue has caused us all manner of problems in the past. It can't continue.*

Seller: *If it did continue and it happened again, how exactly would that hurt you as an organisation?*

Customer: *It would make it impossible for us. My team just wouldn't be able to cope.*

Seller: *So, if you could remove that threat of it happening again, what would it mean to you?*

Customer: *The pressure would be lifted. I believe we would have the ability to hit the timeline laid down by the business.*

Stop asking multi-embedded questions

A multi-embedded question is where a question is added to another question. Salespeople have a tendency to try and use leading/probing-type questions but they add them all together and make it a multi-embedded question.

Seller: *How did that affect you? Did you have people shouting at you? How long did it take to fix it? Are you worried about it happening again?*

Customer: *Yes, I am.*

As with this example, the first, very effective question is smothered by the following three. As a result, the customer gets confused as to which question to answer, and will most likely answer the last one, or if they are a more seasoned executive, will probably answer a totally different question altogether. The amount and quality of information received as a result is diminished.

If you catch yourself doing this, slow down and think before asking your first question (silence helps to create 'presence' and an air of control) and have confidence that your first question is effective. The customer's silence (that you are filling with your subsequent questions) is possibly due to them thinking, as it may have been a question they haven't considered before.

Do your questions engage the brain?

Your role as a salesperson is to get your customer to engage their brain to the point of exploring their issues and challenges they are trying to solve, as well as to emotionally engage them into the solution. You must realise that there are certain ways to do that which can be very effective and other ways that can just as easily turn a customer off your product, no matter how ideal of a fit it is.

Remember, 95% of our decision making is made in the emotional part of our brain, not in the logic. Of course, the product must meet the needs, incorporate the features, etc., but that only gets you to the table. How the customer feels about the you, the solution, how it will affect them personally, will determine if they buy, and if they buy from you. That means that no matter how much logic you pour into a presentation that shows a client how perfect of a fit a product of service is for their business, if they don't have a strong emotional connection to it, they are unlikely to make the purchase – no matter how much of a return on investment you show them.

Brain functionality in questioning

With that in mind, take a look at how the brain functions when you start asking questions.

We have already stated earlier in the book that the brain operates on about 12 watts. To conserve energy, the brain attempts to run on minimal resources and tries not to fire up the engine unless needed. This is how a lot of activities are happening in your brain without any conscious thought – imagine having to remember to breathe in and out constantly!

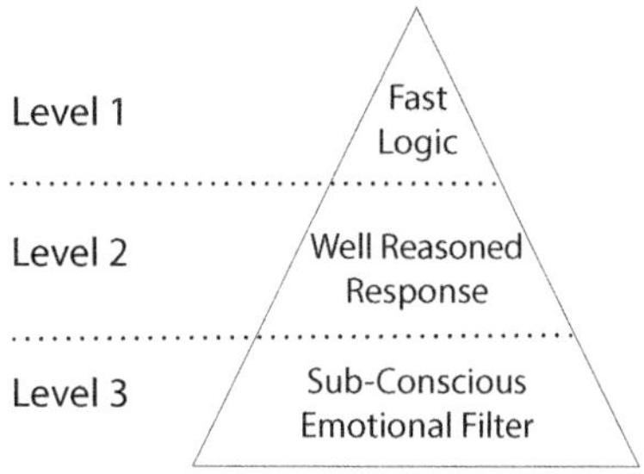

Level 1 – Fast logic
When you ask questions, the customer is likely to give some immediate response – no need to fire up the engine.

> *How many employees do you have?*
> *What markets do you operate in?*
> *What is your revenue target for the next couple of years?*
> *What are your priorities right now?*

All of these questions require little thought from the customer, and they don't need to look for the answer. Even the final question, which is a far-reaching one, won't get the response you really want or need from the customer.

It is the same state as when you walk into the office and say, 'Hi, how are you doing?' The usual and obvious response is 'fine thanks – how are you?'. The brain doesn't fire up as it doesn't think these are necessary taxing questions. Equally, you probably don't think they actually care how you are, and you certainly weren't that interested when you asked. It's this type of thing that has taught the brain to simply respond.

Level 2 – Well-reasoned response
Once the customer has given the 'tip of the tongue' or 'top of the head' response, and you are still showing signs of interest in the answers, then they will move into level 2, and give you a much more well-reasoned response.

The key to access level 2 is to not ask questions on the first thing they say. Use body language, silence or simple affirmations like 'aha' or 'interesting – please go on'. This provides cues for the respondent to continue.

Level 1 is useful, it provides background to the story and may provide some context.

Level 2 provides context and can help you read between the lines and provide subtext to the conversation.

If you ask the customer some bigger questions that require a little more thought, you need to give them time to process it. Some customers will be quite expansive when they talk, others will be a little more thoughtful. Remember the colour personalities we discussed earlier in the book, our extroverted colours, Reds and Oranges, will instantly talk and give you answers and it can take a while for them to get into level 2, whereas our introverted colours, who tend to think before they speak, might get to level 2 a little quicker.

The worst thing a salesperson can do at this point is to dive into the first thing the customer says and try to drill down on it, or worst still, build a solution around it. Let the customer talk, don't guess, don't interrupt, don't blend the story with your own. Let them continue and use body language and affirmations to allow them to know you are listening.

Take notes, as you will need to come back to some of the things that are shared here.

Level 3 – Subconscious

Level 3 is the subconscious mind. In here is the 'why' the person you are talking to has those thoughts and feelings. It is made up of experiences, education, upbringing and everything else that makes a person that person.

Where level 1 gives you context, and level 2 provides the sub-text, level 3 is why the story is the story. It is the emotional filter that is steering the thoughts and feelings of your customer.

The reason it is called the subconscious is because it is below the level of consciousness, i.e. the customer or person you are talking to is unaware of it themselves. The best salespeople, like an awesome therapist, can read between the lines and ask amazing questions to unearth some of these underlining drivers and triggers and steer the customer to a solution that they subconsciously want and need.

Reading level 3 – will enable you to build sales solutions that cover both the logical and emotional mind.

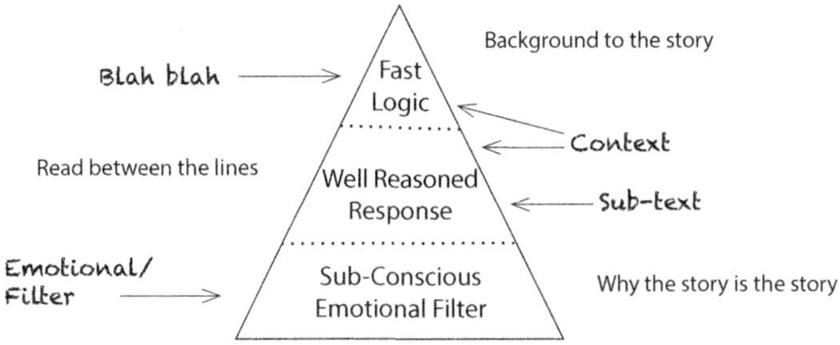

4Q questioning

Understanding that we need to engage the customer's mind and get past the fast logic stage, means that when we are making larger sales and value-based selling, we need our questioning techniques to get through the barriers and have the customer open up and share both business needs and personal needs as well.

The 4Qs are an awesome tool to help you do this. The 4Qs are:

- Background questions
- Problem questions
- Value questions
- Impact questions

These are named to provide instant clarity of what they are about, no need for fancy jargon here.

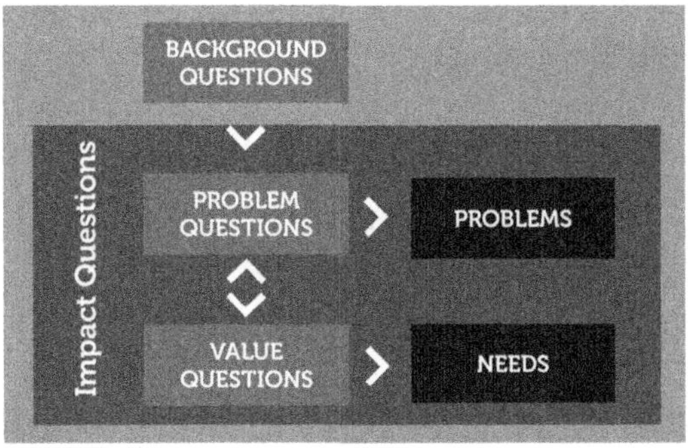

The 4Qs are four very powerful and useful question types that help lead the customer to share their problems and needs that your product and services can solve.

It is not a flow diagram and it is not a process. You can ask any of the questions in any order. Don't feel that you need to get all the background questions out, then all the problems and then move on to value. Conversations are not like that and therefore your questions shouldn't work like that either. Yes, it makes sense to roll on to some as part of the conversation, but do not limit yourself, go with the flow of the conversation but make sure you are influencing the client's mind throughout.

Background questions

Background questions provide just that. They focus on establishing the facts about the company, situation, topic or to confirm some data that may be of interest. Back in the 70s and 80s, background questions were extremely important; how else would you know how many offices they had, what their products and services were and so on? But let's be honest, in the age of the internet and digital technology, a good salesperson should be able to answer most of the questions for themselves before the first meeting ever takes place.

In today's world, the customer expects you to have done your research, and not be asking time-wasting questions. Top sellers today still ask background questions, but usually to clarify some information or to move the customer into a topic they want to explore.

The problem with background questions is that they have little to no influence over the customer's mind. The customer already knows the answers to these questions therefore they the customer can become bored of answering them, and too many can become more of an interrogation then consultation.

Some examples:

> *How many employees do you have?*
> *What's your current labour turnover rate?*
> *What are your strategic priorities at the moment?*

The most important part of background questions is that they need to get to level 2 – a much more well-reasoned response. Don't ask rapid fire questions. Consider TED-type questions that we looked at earlier (tell me, describe to me, explain to me); these will keep your questions down but provide you with lots of data, and get the customer thinking.

Problem questions (building the case for change)

In the book *Insight Selling*, Mike Schultz and John Doerr explain how rather than doing a deep dive needs analysis, as you would have been taught in solution or consultative selling, top salespeople in today's world need to provide insight and lead the customer to the solution. Problem questions, as part of the 4Qs, are designed to do just that. Instead of the facts presented with background questions, the focus of a problem question is to engage the customer's mind and **illicit an opinion or feeling about the problems being faced**. This is how you start to engage the customer emotionally into the sale. It instantly moves the customer into level 2, a more well-reasoned response, and through active listening, you might spot some of level 3 in the answers.

To get your problem questions right you need to utilise feeling-based words and consider using it in a 'leading' question. Utilise words like:

worried	*apprehensive*
nervous	*confident*
afraid	*disappointed*
alarmed	*dissatisfied*
difficult	*doubt*
awkward	*bothered*
frustrated	*annoyed*

To lead the customer to your solution, focus on asking questions that your products and services can fix.

Some example questions are:

How worried are you that your team are wasting too much time on paperwork?
Do you find it difficult finding the information you need?
How frustrating is it that your sales team struggle to build close relationships with you customers?

Value-based questions (moving to a solution mindset)

Since the customer has shared some problems and issues with you, it would be very easy to jump in and start telling the customer how your products and services can fix them, but don't! It's too early.

Psychologically, if you now start talking about the solution, before the customer articulates what they want from the solution, the customer figuratively will sit in judgement on your pitch. In essence you are still leading with the solution. The chances of you getting the pitch right and meeting the image in their mind of what the solution should look like is actually quite remote. You will only create doubt and objections from the customer, not harshly but something like 'Yes, I can see why some people may want that, but …' or 'I'm not sure – that seems a bit more than what I was thinking', just like we explored earlier.

The value questions are important to maintain the customer's involvement in the conversation and move them from talking about negatives (current state) to start thinking about the future and creating all the benefits a solution could bring (future state). It is imperative at this stage to continue to ask questions rather than tell the customer how you can help.

That doesn't mean that you stop influencing the conversation. The answer is to ask loaded questions that plant seeds in their mind about what the solution could potentially look like, and have them tell you all the benefits of having it. In neurological terms we call this 'priming'. By making suggestions, in a collaborative way, you will move the customer into a future-orientated mindset where they mentally build pictures of various attributes of the solution.

Use phrases such as 'if you could …' or 'if you had a way …'

Again, this is a subtle artform. It is not 'If you had our Widget 2000 how would that help?' or 'If you could use our Widget what difference would that make?'. The answer lies in what the feature does, not what it is.

For example, one of our clients sell an HR information system which can do a number of amazing things for their customers. Let's take one of the features of their system which looks after the onboarding process of new hires, a time-consuming aspect of HR as they need to send forms to the new starters requesting all sorts of information from name, address and bank details, references and so on. In addition to this they also need to send out emails to facilities, IT and all those internal services to get them set up with email, building access, laptops, etc. Typical problems customers face are that not all forms come back completed correctly, or passports are out of date, or forms get lost between departments.

Here is an extract of part of the conversation as an example:

> Background Q: *Can you describe to me your current onboarding process of new hires?*
>
> Problem Q: *Are you concerned that your team are wasting too much time chasing up paperwork?*
>
> Customer: *Yes, they can spend ages typing up the letters and following up to get all the information together.*
>
> Value Q: *I see, so if you could automate that process, what difference would that make.*

This value question assumes that the customer wants to solve the problem and moves them to consider the benefits of automated documentation. The customer moves to a future orientation and now tells the salesperson all the benefits they can see from that. The customer knows that the salesperson is obviously asking this question as their product can do that, it is inherent in the conversation, but they can move forward in a more collaborative way rather than sounding too salesy.

Impact questions (building the business case for change)

Impact questions are used to extend the size of the pain or gain. Impact questions can provide metrics and build tangible value to support the three whys (why change, why now and why us). When selling to businesses, and those who are more cost-conscious, building out the impact of the current situation in more tangible terms, and the benefits of the new system, again in tangible terms, will be much easier for your contact to sell to other stakeholders. Value-based selling has been an important aspect in selling to businesses, as well as on more considered purchases, and Gary Gaskill in his 2018 book discusses focusing on business outcomes and value drivers, by asking questions that help them understand the specific factors that drive value for the customer, such as cost savings, revenue growth or risk reduction. This can help the salesperson to demonstrate the value of their solution in terms that are meaningful to the customer.

There are five different areas you could consider drawing impact questions from:

1. Time
2. Money
3. People
4. Workflow/processes
5. Strategy/plans

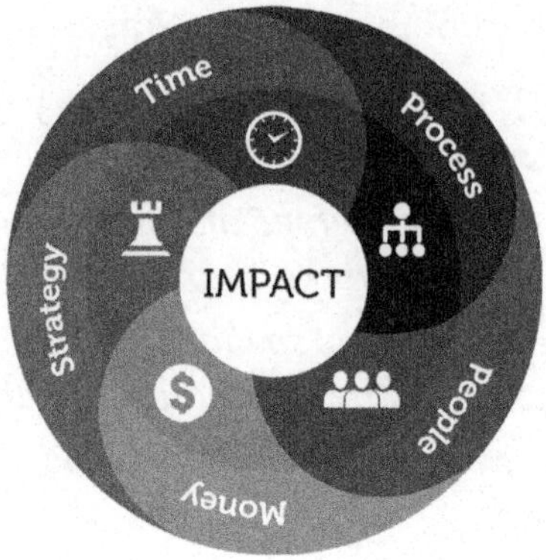

Time and money

Time and money are the most recognisable of the group, and are often the two areas that most salespeople focus on at early stages in the sales process; after all, what business owner or customer does not want to have more time and more money available? If you're selling to someone like the CFO of a company or anyone involved with the bottom line, these are great impact questions to start with.

Once you have a firm handle on what the problem and or needs are, you can delve into ideas such as, 'How much time is it taking?' or 'How much money are you losing because of this issue?'. It is very likely your client has already figured this out internally, and it's one of the chief reasons they are talking to you. The same rules apply for the gain: 'How much time will that give you back?' or 'How much money will that save you?'

However, it's not all as cut and dry as that, because every single one of your competitors is going to pitch in the same two areas: time and money. Make no mistake, these two are extremely valuable commodities to every business, but that does not mean they are the only two out there. If every single company is selling time and money, how do you differentiate yourself from them? The answer is in the other three areas: strategy, people and processes.

People

When considering people as an impact question, you can ask your customer things like: 'Who else is affected by this?' and 'Will that also impact you customers?' Very rarely is a problem or benefit limited to just one part of your company. The more people that has impacted, the bigger the problem and the higher priority it will become to get it solved as soon as possible. A cut on the finger can be covered up with a bandage; a wound that is bleeding from five different spots needs immediate attention.

In addition, impact on other people, especially customers, gets the ear of different people in an organisation. If you contact is going to need additional sign off, other members of the leadership team will be more prone to listen and take action if it affects customers.

Process

Consider the impact in terms of processes or workflow. Does the problem or need have additional impacts on these elements of the business? Depending on your products and services, this might have a larger or lesser of an impact, but when you start looking at what is affected you will be surprised at how you can extend the size of the pain and gain into these areas. Consider what areas are being held up, what blockages occur, will this help streamline certain aspects of the workflow? Below is an example of workflow and processes issues from the previous example for the HR system provider.

Strategy

Strategy questions could involve asking what other projects are being delayed, shelved or cancelled because of the problem at hand, or what are the future goals and objectives and how will this impact those going forward. This is a far-reaching question that might not immediately be apparent depending on the level of responsibility of the person you are engaging with. You could ask, 'What is this stopping you from doing?'

Asking impact questions helps the customer realise that the problem is much bigger than it appears on the surface and can move it to a more strategic conversation rather than tactical. This is the platform on which you will build the case for change, which is the linchpin in getting a customer to pull the trigger and make the decision to buy.

True value-based selling will require you to link your solution at multiple levels of the organisation, such as: business objectives, how does this attribute to the organisations strategic objectives, departmental objectives, how does it actually help, and KPIs, how does it help achieve and deliver real performance metrics?

Functional objectives

Let's go back to our HR software example earlier, this time with the impact questions added:

> Background Q: *Can you describe to me your current onboarding process of new hires?*
>
> Problem Q: *Are you concerned that your team are wasting too much time chasing up paperwork?*
>
> Customer: *Yes, they can spend ages typing up the letters and follow up to get all the information together.*
>
>> Impact Q: *What negative impact does that have on the new hires?*
>>
>> Impact Q: *If the paperwork is late coming back, does that affect any other departments?*
>>
>> Impact Q: *Because they are sales hires, does that have a knock-on effect in terms of sales targets and revenue?*
>
> Value Q: *I see, so if you could automate that process, what difference would that make?*
>
>> Impact Q: *How much time do you think that would save?*
>>
>> Impact Q: *Would that also help with your future recruitment drive?*
>>
>> Impact Q: *And what about employee engagement – would you see that go up for your own team and that of new recruits?*

On the face of it, questions are simple, ask the customer what they want and give it to them. Yes, if you want to be an average salesperson! Top salespeople know that you can use questions to lead the customer to believe they are engineering a solution which just so happens to be exactly what they are selling!

Metrics are more than ROI

Building metrics is more than providing a return on investment. When you become more engaged in the conversation with the customer and the conversations turn to be more about the impact of the solution, you change the dynamic of the sale and your relationship.

Building champions

One of the aspects in business to business (b2b) sales is that the person you are dealing with more often will need to sell the solution internally to the other stakeholders. Working through the impact, and building out the metrics, provides them with the tools they need to gain buy-in to the solution, but also moves you into more of a coaching relationship. You are helping build out their personal wins and therefore reinforcing your relationships.

Move from tactical to strategic

Focusing on the impacts of the solution, rather than the features and operation of the product, migrates the sale from being a tactical purchase, or a product acquisition, to a strategic project that impacts not only the department but far wider across the business. It changes the conversation from being about what to do to fix things today, to a longer, future-focused perspective.

Shift from price to value

The focus also moves away from price and how much it costs, to the value the business will gain from having the solution, both in terms of the removal of the pain and benefits they will gain. Value will be measured differently by different departments, and therefore remember to utilise a variety of impact questions.

Opens doors

Having metrics will raise interest in a lot more people than the person you are dealing with. Yes, the Economic Buyer will be interested, but also so will a wider audience, both within the existing customers' business and for your other prospects. When you want to get higher and wider across the existing organisation, these metrics will be important to demonstrate the impact you have had already, and doors will suddenly be open to you, as people will want to learn more.

Put the customer into a buying mindset

In the connect part of the sale, you were building rapport and allowing the customer to feel comfortable with you to be open to exploring their wants and needs.

In a more assisted sale, or on those larger deals that you have been working on, after you have engaged the customer, you moved on and asked some great questions to explore their problems and needs.

In the explore part of the sale we focused on creating two mindsets:

1. Inquisitive mindset – where they shared some of their problems and challenges.
2. Solution mindset – where they were open to consider potential solutions that would help overcome their problems and provide additional benefits.

The focus now is to move them into a buying mindset. The idea here is not only to put the customer into a position to be able to *make* a decision, but also to *take* the decision – which might sound a bit gimmicky but are actually two different things as we will show you going forward.

Putting the customer into a buying mindset starts back at the questioning techniques and asking the questions that led the customer to the solution (not lead with). Feel free to go back and read that section again. The reality here is that the customer is going to need to be sure that this is what they want and need, and that it adds value (back to the section on loss aversion).

The value proposition

Value propositions come in two kinds, those that attract the left brain thinking, where we create our rational arguments, and those that attract the right brain thinking, where our emotional arguments are conjured up. We've talked extensively about how powerful emotions can be in deciding on whether or not to purchase. But we also know from our four colour types that people are going to go about their processes in a particular way before those decisions are made. For the Salecology Reds and Blues of the world, a methodical decision-making process is the only way to get to the proper decision. For these types, our value proposition needs to make financial sense, business sense, and markedly improve the situation from how it is now. For the Salecology Orange and Greens, the emotions will also be super charged as you start presenting the solution to gain their buy-in.

Before we get to show you how to gain buy-in from the customer and put them into a buying mindset, there are a couple of Salecology aspects to share:

Leading not pacing
Everything we have been speaking about previously concerning matching and mirroring has been designed for you to get into rapport and maintain it by mirroring the customer. This is called pacing. Once you have rapport, and find you are mirroring each other, you can start to take the lead and have the customer follow your body language and tonal patterns. This is called leading. Your positive body language, such as nodding and affirming gestures, will be important to continue to reinforce the confidence in the solution.

Removal of doubt and complexity
If the customer has doubt in their mind, or questions they feel have not yet been answered, they probably won't be able to take a decision just yet. You will need to help them in your demonstration, presentation or summary to remove the complexity from the sale and remove any doubt. Think of the customer having a checklist in their mind and when you present your final solution, they will need to check it off as you go through it. If things are not clear or remain unchecked, then don't expect a decision to take place. If you can have them mentally tick it off as you go through your presentation, then their mind can be made up and take the decision to go ahead.

Hypnotic language

I have loved the study of hypnotism and enjoy the work of Milton Erickson, Paul McKenna, and the showmanship of Derren Brown. This book isn't going to teach you how to hypnotise your customers into signing orders, that's not ethically acceptable, but it will show you how to use language patterns that hypnotists use and how the power of suggestion works. If you understand that, you can modify the way you present your solutions to gain much better acceptance and have more people say 'yes' to you.

Unquestionable truths

The first part of putting someone into an agreeable state, is to put the brain into a position where it accepts what is being said is the truth. To do this you must tell it things which are unquestionable true. A hypnotherapist utilises the power of three to start to put you into a trance state and it follows a pattern as follows:

Step 1: Tell the patient three unquestionable truths to put their mind into a rest state (stop the inner dialogue from questioning) and then suggest what you want the mind to start to absorb

Step 2: Tell the patient two more unquestionable truths; this mixes the suggestion into the camp of the truths.

Step 3: Make the repeated suggestion, followed by another truth to embed it.

If performed correctly, with the right amount of confidence and verbal tones, the patient will now be open to suggestion and their mind will be focused on the suggested topic.

The hypnotic heartbeat

Linking all the things above, pacing and leading and hypnotic language, means you can make benefit statements with more influence to gain customers' approval and confirmation that what they are seeing is useful and adds value to them. If you have completed your 4Q questioning correctly you will have an even stronger way to present your solution and move the customer into a decision-taking mindset. Using the hypnotic heartbeat process, we can move the customer into a positive, solution-based mindset that makes them more interested in buying.

Done correctly, this process removes doubt, questioning and gets the customer to say yes.

Like an actual human heartbeat, there's an up and down flow to the hypnotic heartbeat rather than a straight line. This emphasises the tonality you need to use and where the focus of your energy should be.

The process starts with a need you have uncovered. Here you relay back to the customer what they have established as their need and why they need it.

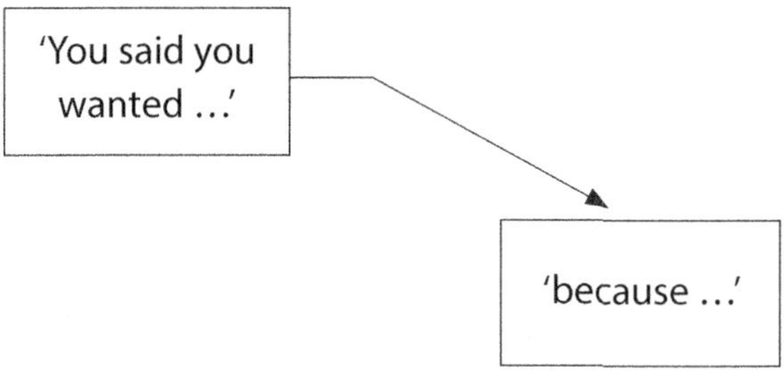

It starts with an opening such as 'You said you wanted to be able to …'. This is you replaying their need and reinforcing the fact that it is not you that is suggesting it to them, it is reconfirmation that they said they want it. Straight after that you reinforce the problems and negative impacts that led them to want or need it.

Tonality and the power of three

It is important to lower your voice when you replay the problems, dissatisfactions and negative impacts. When people talk about painful things, empathy kicks in and everyone tends to lower their voice and demonstrates some mutual concern. As you get into the reaffirmation of the need and why they need it, utilise the power of three, and replay two or three things about what they have said about the problem and impact. This therefore becomes unquestionable because you are only replaying what they have said to you.

Don't stop midway!

Don't embellish, add your own opinion, or go off on a tangent at this point. If you do, then they cease to be unquestionable truths and you will lose the flow and change the mindset of the customer. Some people ask a question at this point to try and gain confirmation that this is correct

– don't! If you stop after the painful aspects, you will take the customer back to the inquisitive mindset and they may now start talking about other painful things or reliving the issues and you will be back into the explore/discovery aspect of the sale.

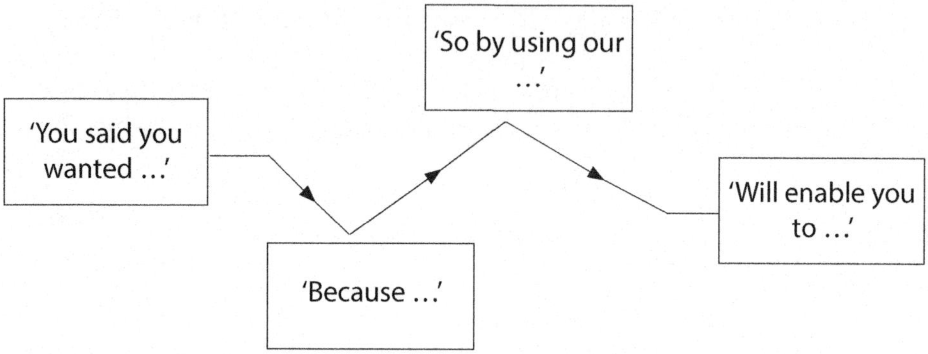

Don't skip a beat

The third step is to bounce upward with your tonal patterns, energy and volume. This is setting the scene of the happier place to be, the answer to their needs, by telling them the feature or service that will solve the problem. This, as you saw in the hypnotic language paragraph, is the moment you are making the suggestion – 'So by using our …'.

You also saw in the hypnotic language that you need to follow up again with some more truths for the brain to accept the sequence. This is where you follow up with the benefits already uncovered during your value questions and positive impact questions.

'So, by using our … will enable you to …'

The tonal pattern in the benefit statements comes back to neutral. The ear will pick up on the tonal level and it will reinforce the confidence and stability in the benefits. To ensure these stick, remember the power of three – you should be able to reinforce the benefits with more than a one-liner, present back three benefits the customer told you during your 4Q questioning.

Confirmation and gaining buy-in

To complete the cycle, we need the customer to confirm in their mind that they agree with the statement. This verbal confirmation is much more than confirming that you have got it right. If the customer says out loud that they agree, understand why you are showing them the feature, or why you are recommending it, it tells their mind that this is correct and turns off the inner voice of doubt.

Before you move onto the next heartbeat, with another feature, or are going to conduct the demonstration, get confirmation and affirmation that the customer understands that this is what they are looking for.

Pulling it together

The power of the heartbeat is that it removes the ability for the customer to object. You are not selling anything in this heartbeat, simply telling them the feature that will give them the answers to what they are after. You have shown empathy, you have shown that you listen, and you are now showing them how to solve the problem.

To bring this to life and link it back to your questioning techniques, let's pull it together with the example used at the end of the 4Qs and the HR software company:

> Problem Q: *Are you concerned that your team are wasting too much time chasing up paperwork?*
>
> Customer: *Yes, they can spend ages typing up the letters and following up to get all the information together.*
>
> Impact Q: *What negative impact does that have on the new hires?*
>
> Customer: *It can slow down the joining date and it's not really a great experience.*
>
> Impact Q: *If the paperwork is late coming back, does that affect any other departments?*
>
> Customer: *Sometimes the paperwork can get missed and puts more pressure on HR Ops to keep chasing it.*
>
> Impact Q: *Because they are sales hires, does that have a knock-on effect in terms of sales targets and revenue?*
>
> Customer: *The targets don't change even if they are short of salespeople, but empty seats on the sales floor has a direct impact on revenue and performance. I know the team are struggling this year with some lofty sales goals.*

Value Q: *I see, so if you could automate that process, what difference would that make?*

Customer: *Of course that would be useful, it would free us up to focus more on the value-added work and business partnering, then admin.*

Impact Q: *How much time do you think that would save?*

Customer: *I don't know how much time really, but it would definitely save a lot.*

Impact Q: *Would that also help with your future recruitment drive?*

Customer: *It would make them run smoother, and with a potential of 100+ new hires this year, it would streamline the process and ensure we didn't miss out on candidates, plus speed up onboarding.*

Impact Q: *And what about employee engagement – would you see that go up for your own team and that of new recruits?*

Customer: *Definitely, the team already complain about the paper trail, so automating this will allow them to get on with the parts of the job they enjoy, and the recruits themselves will get a much better experience.*

Accepting this part of the conversation will be a small element of the whole conversation, but let us show the heartbeat based on this aspect:

You said you wanted to automate the onboarding process because …

(Tonal pattern goes down)

The team are taking ages typing up and chasing up paperwork which is:

- *slowing down joining dates*
- *paperwork can get missed and then needs chasing later on*
- *which is also having an impact on the sales team, who have some lofty sales targets this year*

(Tonal pattern goes right up)

So by using our pre-boarding workflow will enable you to:

(Tonal pattern returns to neutral)

- *save a lot of time by streamlining the process*

- *enable the team to focus on more value-adding work, increasing engagement in the team*
- *and get new hires onboard while providing a much better experience*

Can you see why this is an important part to include in the software?

The customer is going to struggle to say no at this point.

Depending on what you sales style is, some people prefer to run through three heartbeats and then go into a demonstration of the three features, while others may do a heartbeat then show the feature, then do the next heartbeat and then show the feature and so on. Both ways work. The main point is don't stop in the middle of a heartbeat when summarising. You want the customer to say yes before showing it.

Adapt sales presentations to make sense

Having looked at several aspects of psychology and how to engage the customer both emotionally and mentally, let's look at how the customer's brain operates and how it makes sense of the world around it. By understanding how it receives and processes information, and how it comes to conclusions, we can adapt our sales presentations, demonstrations and negotiations to make perfect sense to their brain.

Filters and representational systems

OK, let's look at the science first: representational systems and filters are two related concepts in the field of cognitive psychology. Representational systems refer to the different ways in which people process and represent information in their minds, while filters refer to the unconscious processes that people use to selectively attend to and process incoming information.

Representational systems are the more scientific term for our internal senses. Everyone knows about our five senses – sight, sound, touch, smell and taste. These all gather in our brain and dictate how we remember things, how we describe things, and how we ultimately communicate things. Different people tend to have different preferences for processing information, with some individuals relying more heavily on visual information, others on auditory information, and still others on kinaesthetic information (more physical sensations).

Neurolinguistic programme (NLP), brought to us by Grinder and Bandler, evolved their thinking on these systems in that late 70s and showed how people can anchor different experiences, including smell and taste, to particular emotions. Understanding people's representational system can be useful for improving learning and memory, as well as for tailoring communication to the preferences of others.

Filters are unconscious processes that people use to selectively process incoming information. These filters are influenced by factors such as past experiences, beliefs, values and attitudes, and can cause people to process information that is consistent with their existing beliefs and to ignore or discount information that is inconsistent with their beliefs. Filters can also cause people to selectively attend to certain aspects of incoming information while ignoring other aspects. Consider why you think the way you do. What has made you think like that? Your filter is determined by your 'map of the world' and some areas include:

- childhood and upbringing
- schooling and education level
- social class
- religion
- life experiences
- Past decisions
- Travel
- Political environment
- Age
- Financial stability

One important filter is the confirmation bias, which is the tendency to seek out and interpret information in a way that confirms pre-existing beliefs and to ignore or discount information that contradicts those beliefs. Reinforced by Raymond Nickerson's book in 1998, it can lead to a reinforcement of existing beliefs, even in the face of contradictory evidence.

Understanding the role of representational systems and filters can be useful in a variety of contexts, including education, communication and interpersonal relationships. By understanding your own representational system and the filters that influence the way you process information, you can improve their ability to learn and communicate effectively with others. Additionally, recognising the representational systems and filters of your customers and clients will enable you to tailor your communication to the preferences and biases of others, improving your ability to connect, build positive relationships and tailor your demonstrations and pitches to land and 'make sense' in the customer's brain.

Brain operating system (cognitive styles)

Consider you brain as a computer and it needs an operating system to store, recall or process information. Much like iOS, Linux or Windows, let's call this our bOS, our brain operating system. Our bOS runs on one of three representational systems – visual, audio or physical. Each of us has a preference for how we receive data best and how we talk about that data. Some people are visually orientated (visual), some are sound orientated (audio) orientated, and some are kinaesthetically oriented, which is the scientific word for emotional feeling or touch – we will call this the physical, (NLP call it kinaesthetic).

We continually make use of our sensory systems, switching between one to another for different reasons throughout the day. Most people, however, tend to favour one over the others and therefore process most of their information in the preferred manner. Some might have an even blend across two but a lot less common is a balance across all three. But remember, this is all done unconsciously.

By knowing your primary sensory preference, and that of your customer, you can adapt your sales style, presentation and pitch, to communicate directly to their brain and engage both their conscious and unconscious mind. This will mean they will be more receptive to your ideas and influences.

Visual operating system

The visual operating system is a great one. Those running this operating system **SEE** the world. They process data in a visual way, they picture things in their mind, and use visual types of words – 'I see what you mean, I'm looking for some bright ideas.' They also store memories in a pictorial format, so when they recall things, you will notice they describe past events and experiences in a visual context.

Visual system processing means someone prefers using their eyes for memory and decision making. Their vision is their main contact to the world at large. For these people, pictures are more powerful than sounds or feelings. This also means they are better at long-range planning and seeing the bigger picture. Various researchers of NLP have identified famous of people who relied heavily on visual system processing such as:

Leonardo da Vinci's	drawings are some of the most famous representations of science in human history.
Walt Disney	was famous for visualising his creations as drawings and cartoons, but also for developing massive scale models of theme parks that would not be completed until after his death.
Albert Einstein	was able to visualise concepts that could not be seen with the naked eye, thus giving us the most famous equation, that for mass-energy

	equivalence, and also developing the theory of relativity, which introduced the theory of spacetime.
Mozart	is perhaps a surprise entry in this category, but studies of his work and writings indicate that he was able to see completed works of music in his head, then able to transcribe them onto paper.
Steve Jobs	the late co-founder and CEO of Apple, was known for his visual and design-oriented approach to product development and marketing.

Other visual clues that show that someone has a preference for visual processing include:

- They are better at remembering faces than they are with names.
- They would rather talk to your face or on a video call than talk via phone or text so that they can better understand what you mean via your facial reactions.
- They see a lot more information in a picture rather than a verbal description of something.
- They often need a picture or some other visualisation to understand what you are saying, especially if it is a concept they are previously unfamiliar with.
- If there is a lot of physical activity going on all in one place, they might have a hard time being able to concentrate.
- They need space to see the pictures in their minds. If you talk on top of them while they are doing this, you can interrupt their thought process (or they can't hear you).
- They are much more in tune with how they look, how their homes look and how others look.
- They often talk more quickly than other people, breathe at a faster rate and have tension in their upper bodies while communicating as they sometimes struggle to translate into words what is so clear in their mind's eye.

When it comes to talking to clients or customers, realising someone is strongly attuned with the visual representation internally allows you to use patterns of speech that appeal to that sense and get you on the same wavelength with them.

Visuals use words like:

I see	*looks good*	*bright idea*	*show me*
perceive	*picture*	*highlight*	*focus*
reflect	*clear*	*illustrate*	*watch*

Asking a visual person questions such as 'What does look like to you?' and 'Can you highlight some of the key challenges you see over the next quarter?' are ideal ways to captivate their attention and allow their brain to both receive and relay information in its preferred way.

If you are working with someone who is running a visual bOS you need to consider your various communications for them to quickly connect and get the information you are sharing. Below are some things to consider:

Images and pictures	If a picture paints a thousand words make sure you use imagery in your slides, presentations and material.
Graphs and diagrams	As with images, a visual preference wants graphical depictions of the information; this will help the see the data more clearly.
Video and video calls	Utilising video content and video calling is more stimulating and your customer will be more engaged in the data and correspondence. You will notice the visuals leave their cameras on more than the others.
Colours and fonts	Don't be shy of using colour, highlights and fonts to bring the content to life. Even in an email, you can draw the attention with good use of colour.
Glossy handouts and PDFs	Consider the material that you send. Visuals will prefer a nice glossy finish or well-presented PDF with graphics.
Clean slides	Don't overpower the slides with too much content and data. For visuals, less is more – remember a picture paints a thousand

	words, so use short text, a few bullet points, and don't over animate.
Personal presentation	Attire and grooming is essential, check the shoes you are wearing are clean, if your shirt is well pressed, your laptop bag is bursting and so on. They will also look behind you in the video call to see what's on the shelf. In addition to this, they also will want to see you be a little animated and therefore will be looking at hand gestures, facial expressions.

Audio operating system

The audio bOS is also extremely powerful. Those running this programming language **HEAR** the world. They process data based on whether it sounds right and use soundbites to access information stored in their memory to recall whether they have heard it before and whether it resonates with them.

Auditory system processing refers to the words being said as well as the tonal aspects including tone, pace, pitch and volume. Tone can have a huge impact on whether the customer will take you seriously or not. Tone of voice is a vital part of communication before we can even understand words. Babies can grasp who is talking to them and can be soothed by a tone of voice. They take comfort in this and know when someone is happy with them. Animals are the same way. You might think your dog can differentiate between the words for going outside, having a snack and being allowed to jump on the couch, but it has a lot more to do with the tone of voice you use to say these words to them.

That being said, some individuals who are known for their auditory orientation in their communication and thinking styles and have been associated with the audio preference include:

Martin Luther King Jr.	The civil rights leader was known for his powerful and persuasive speeches, which often made use of repetition, rhythm and other auditory techniques to engage his audience.
Barack Obama	The former US president was known for his

	eloquence and use of language in his speeches, which often featured rhythmic and melodic elements.
Oprah Winfrey	The media mogul and talkshow host is known for her skilful use of language and her ability to connect with her audience through her voice and tone.

Being particularly attuned to audible data often inclines a person to do well with musical ability or writing poetry. But it's not always about success in the arts. Mechanics who work on a host of different vehicles can often hear when something is out of place in an engine or a mechanical system before they ever do any sort of diagnostic with a computer.

If you want to be able to understand if your customer is inclined to auditory system representation, you can also look for these behaviours:

- They are more apt to want to talk on the phone rather than face to face (no need for the video call).
- They get locked into listening to the point.
- They do not notice changes around them visually.
- They are distracted by noises that interfere with their flow of events.
- They will ask many questions and like to talk out problems whenever possible.
- Their breathing is deep and reaches their diaphragm.
- They talk at a medium pace and their voice often carries resonance.
- While they enjoy talking and listening to music, they also very much appreciate a quiet environment – the lack of sound can be as appealing as sound itself.

As described earlier, people running an audio bOS will also interpret the world in audio and therefore will utilise sound-based words in their speech patterns:

sounds good	*rings a bell*	*I'm all ears*	*have you heard*
tell me	*say*	*mention*	*ask*
remark	*express*	*resonate*	*talk*

When talking to this sort of customer about problems and solutions, use questions such as 'How does that sound?' or 'You mentioned earlier about xyz, tell me more about that'. These questions can appeal to them specifically by letting them know you are on the same wavelength, and that you are listening and interested to hear more.

Quite often with audio preferences you would hear them say something like, 'OK, slow down, sit down and talk me through it'. Below are some other hints and tips on how to adjust your engagement with the audio bOS to get faster connections and to resonate better with this type of audience.

Word patterns

One of the things I was always taught in presentation skills was 'tell them what you were going to tell them', 'tell them' 'and then tell them what you told them'. Throughout your presentation make sure that you use the same word patterns and keep repeating the same message.

Slogans, catchphrases and rhyme

When we hear certain sounds or slogans we can instantly and rhyme recognise the brand, e.g. the phrase 'just do it' is synonymous with the brand Nike. To make your presentation or demonstration more memorable, make sure that you utilise a project name for the proposal and or repeat phrases or slogans throughout the presentation. Audio preferences also remember rhyming words so try to consider that as part of the deck.

Tonality

Pace, pitch, tone and volume are all key things to consider when communicating with the audio preference. But as highlighted above, ensuring that the rhythm of your speech, as well as the acoustics of your voice, will also have an important part in how the information is received. Make sure you utilise emphasis to stress important aspects of your proposal, e.g. when talking about something meaningful, lowering one's voice invokes a different meaning than when one raises their voice in excitement or anticipation.

Precision

One of the important things is to ensure that what you say is accurate, precise and most importantly that it sounds correct. The audio operating system accesses the brain to check if it has heard what you are saying before and whether it sounds right. Therefore, if you are unsure about what you are saying, it is better to refer back than guess or make up some answer.

The power of three

It seems strange at this part of the book to suddenly change direction a little, however, I think it's important to share with you the power of three as it is very important for the audio brain operating system but also extremely powerful in any communication. I also made mention of it earlier in the use of hypnotic language, and also in the pain and gain aspects of FABs.

The power of three, sometime referred to as the rule of three, is a principle that suggests that things that come in threes are more satisfying, effective and memorable than other numbers. The origins of this principle are not entirely clear, but it has been observed and utilised in various fields and cultures throughout history.

One possible explanation is based on the way the human brain processes information. Research has shown that the brain is better able to remember and process information in groups of three than in larger or smaller groups. This is known as chunking, a process by which the brain organises information into meaningful units that can be easily remembered and processed.

The human brain is somehow programmed to enjoy and understand things in threes. In storytelling we're always shared stories which include the number three, *the three blind mice, the three little pigs, Goldilocks and the three bears, the Three Amigos, the Three Musketeers, Huey, Dewey and Louie and so.* The human brain also seems to remember things in threes, for example when we remember phone numbers we seem to recall them in three digits, we learn our ABCs, we learn to count 1, 2, 3. Knowing that the brain likes three, and remembers things in threes, it's an important factor to therefore deliver your message and communication utilising the power of three.

When you start off your speech or presentation, and you say something like 'I've come here today to talk about three things' the audience will instantly sit up and take notice and look forward to those three things. If you said, 'I've came in today to talk about these five things', it just seems a little bit unwieldy and not as exciting. Equally, when someone says 'I just have a couple of things to share', it somehow seems less important.

Consider your slide show, presentation, or a meeting agenda. Quite often item 1 is about introductions or some summary, and item 5 is possibly agreeing next steps or conclusion. If you took those things off the agenda slide, it will be three interesting points. Now as you go through the presentation or meetings make sure you signpost the three things, and as you recap at the end of the meeting, the customer/audience will remember those three points and you have succeeded in delivering the core messages. Even consider the project name, if it has three words people will remember it more – think Nike's slogan, (Just Do It), or McDonald's (I'm Lovin It).

Physical operating system

The physical operating system loves to **touch and feel things**, it's emotionally charged and therefore wants things to be tangible and real. This operating system uses physical words like 'it doesn't feel right, I need something more robust, give me a concrete example'. The physical system therefore wants to be **hands-on and based on reality**.

In NLP (neurolinguistic programming) this system is referred to as kinaesthetic, however, in Salecology we tend to bring touch, feel and feelings into play. These feelings can be quite different from simply considering emotions, which are more evaluations put together by our brains. Sensations come from the sensory receptors located in our joints, tendons, muscles and our inner ear; visceral sensations are functions of our organs and can be manifested in the likes of hunger and thirst; and tactile sensations, which are things we feel through our skin such as temperature, pressure, pain and texture.

Here are a few more examples of individuals who have been associated with the physical, or kinaesthetic modality in NLP:

Princess Diana	The late Princess of Wales was known for her empathy, compassion and physical touch, which she often used to connect with others.
Mother Teresa	The Catholic nun and humanitarian was known for her physical presence and her ability to convey love and compassion through her touch and physical gestures.
Arnold Schwarzenegger	The former bodybuilder and actor is known for his physical strength, discipline, and ability to control and manipulate his body in various ways.
Michael Jordan	The former professional basketball player is known for his physical agility, athleticism and ability to manipulate his body in ways that allowed him to perform incredible feats on the court.

This version of the operating system is usually slower than auditory and visual when it comes to processing, as there are a lot of different 'moving parts' at play.

If you suspect someone is a physical processor, you can look for the following signs, including:

- They experience things by doing and often have trouble learning by traditional teaching methods (look and listen).
- They pay close attention to their bodies and how they are physically feeling.
- They are tactile and get a lot of information from that touch. They also tend to have something in their hands at any given time, they will play with their pen, flick through papers, grab something off the desk.
- They would rather wear clothes and shoes that are comfortable rather than those that look good or are in the latest fashion.
- They make decisions based on how they are feeling.
- They talk more slowly as it takes time to transcribe their feelings into words.

The physical bOS needs to have it in their hand for it to be real and therefore it is much more interested in the 'here and now' than looking too far into the future and 'what could be'. This also manifests itself in the use of language:

concrete	*touch base*	*good grasp*	*grab me*
feel	*tap into*	*tackle*	*know*
impress upon	*intuit*	*handle*	*suffer*

You would no doubt have heard people processing via the physical system when you hear sayings like 'I need something more concrete', 'let's touch base next week', 'I don't know, it just doesn't grab me' or 'let's tackle this together'.

As much as we want to put something in their hand, which is imperative if we want them to buy it, it is also important to note that they also want things to be pragmatic and real and can start lacking interest quickly if we move to abstract thinking. Here are some things to consider when selling to the physical bOS.

Send it in the post

Rather than just sending an email and a PDF, the physical people enjoy holding the paper or the book or the brochure in the hand. What you tend to find is even if you send something as an attachment, the physical bOS needs to print it out and prefers to thumb through the document. Also, if you have a sample product or example of the solution, sending it to them so they have it in the hand will lead to a greater connection to the product or service and makes it tangible.

Give them the pen

Another great tip for people that are physical is to get them physically involved. Rather than you write on the whiteboard why not give them the pen and ask them to write the notes or capture the ideas. What is fascinating to observe is that they write some things on the board and not others. This will not be done consciously but probably more a subconscious behaviour as they will agree or disagree with some of the ideas being tabled at the meeting. The fact that they have the pen in their hand means that they feel empowered to engage in the conversation and lead some of it and at the same time enables you to facilitate and steer the conversation rather than capture the notes.

Site visits and face to face We know that the physical preference can get more for the handshake than 100 words being said and therefore having a face-to-face meeting is important. Equally having the customer do a site visit or come to your office will provide a lot more confidence in you, your business and your solution.

You steer, I'll navigate One of the things I often see people get wrong is on product demonstrations. All too often the salesperson wants to show the customer all the features and benefits of the product. This may work for a visual, but the physical preference needs to touch and feel the product themselves, hence after the demo they request trials and test drive, etc. Why not say, 'you drive, I'll navigate'. For example, on a software demonstration give them the control of the mouse and keyboard and you tell them where to click and type. This will give the customer much more confidence in the product and they'll get a feel for how easy it is to use.

Pre-work activity and collaboration As we move more towards doing business over the phone or on video calls, one of the ways to get the customer to be more engaged is to ask them to prepare some content or information for the meeting. Having them physically involved in the run-up to the meeting will ensure that they are more involved in the meeting. You can also increase their participation by inviting them to host the meeting or at least present in it. Also in larger groups, utilise breakout rooms for more hands-on collaboration.

Feelings-based questions

In the questioning technique chapter previously we discussed utilising feelings-based verbs to emotionally engage the customer in the conversation. Feelings-based words such as are you worried, do you find it difficult, is it frustrating, are much more important for the physical brain operating system.

Dealing with larger groups

As you start practising these behaviours and spotting customer preferences it will become easier. So, it goes without saying that when you don't know which person has which preference it becomes imperative that you adapt your presentation style to utilise all three preferences. This is also true when selling to larger groups as there will be a combination of visual audio and physical preferences within it.

My experience is that when making presentations or demonstrations, ensuring that your slideshow is visually appealing and that your grooming is not distracting for the visuals is the first step. Secondly, consider your tonality and use of voice as you deliver the presentation. Ensure that you utilise the power of three within your slides and signpost them as you go through them. Use a catchy phrase or rhyme as a name for the project; this will be important to resonate with the audios. Thirdly, make sure that your presentation is interactive and you're asking the audience to partake in the conversation. I have found that a quiz, a whiteboard exercise or pausing for some challenging questions to the audience (not just from the audience) enables the physicals to become more involved. Glossy and colourful handouts, sweets and cakes, and breakout groups are all great tools to involve all three of the preferences.

Negotiate the close

There is a thought that used to be taught in the old sales training which says, the more objections you get the closer you are closing. Really? No! This is just some relic from those days of spray and pray, meaning that if they are still talking to you and haven't walked away yet, then there is a still a chance of closing.

In reality, you must consider what is going on in the mind of the customer. An objection could be genuine, or it could be a negotiation tactic, or it could mean that the customer is unsure, or have some level of doubt in their mind. Whichever it is, the emotionally intelligent person needs to understand what is happening in the customer's mind and help them resolve the conflict in their head and come to a decision.

Wrong reactions

Firstly, you should understand that it is easier to agree then disagree. It takes less effort to say yes than it does to say no. Saying no means that you must conjure up extra inner strength to figuratively repel the other person. You know what I mean if your loved one or child looks you in the eyes and says 'PLLEEEAAASSSEEE'. It is hard to say no, even if no is completely the right thing.

Interestingly, when someone disagrees with a statement it breaks rapport. This breakage of rapport between the customer and the seller has all sorts of outcomes. For the less experienced, that breakage of rapport triggers the fight-or-flight response in the brain, and they immediately look to try and regain rapport by either:

Flight let me go away and take another look at the proposal and see what I can do.

Fight yes but you don't understand Mr Customer, this proposal is …

We sometimes also see the change in relationship from the adult-to-adult relationship to a more subservient nature where the seller becomes like a lost puppy trying to get the customer to like them again.

Subservient	*what if I could do a better price, what if I could offer a better term, what if I could speak to my boss, what can I do, etc.*

It's almost like begging for forgiveness and I'll do anything for you to like me again.

Where is the objection coming from?

The better reaction to objections is to understand that the objection is coming from either a rational place or a more emotional place.

1. Does your product or service meet the customer's needs better than, or at least as good as, the alternatives. This includes features and benefits, price, availability, etc. This is a logical aspect and review of your product mix.
2. Does the customer actually want it, like it, i.e. how do they feel about it.

Most sales development gurus will tell you that objection prevention is better than handling the objection. Wow, what insight, I'm sure you never thought about that before they said it! We have covered off earlier in the book the key aspects of features, advantages and benefits. Now is a good time to remind you of some of the outcomes when you sell on the wrong things.

1. Selling on features leads to price objections.
2. Selling on advantages leads to general objections.

Therefore, if you want to prevent getting price objections stop selling on features, if you want to stop getting other objections, focus more on your exploring and the 4Qs (effective questioning chapter) to build benefit statements, not advantages.

'And' instead of 'but'

Let's look deeper into dealing with the objections. We said earlier that it takes more energy for a customer to object than it does to agree with you. Therefore, knowing that they have had to use more energy to reject you they will now be on their guard ready for the fight that is probably about to ensue.

To explore this further, let's look at the way people present their objections. It normally includes the word 'but'. The saying will be something like, 'I understand what you are saying but …' or often it is 'yes, but …' and then after the 'but' is the objection. The word 'but' means no. Even 'yes, but' means 'no'!

Let's take a simple scenario and see how our brains pick up on the word. You are with a group of friends and someone says:

> *Hey, we could go into town tonight, grab a few drinks and have dinner at the Italian.*
>
> Another friend says, *Yeah we could do that but we could also go and see the new movie that has just come out.*

Essentially, the word 'but' signifies 'yes we could do your idea, but my idea is better'. Even if it is not meant with malice, our brains pick up on the fact that it is an alternative option. We also see this play out in many team meetings, brainstorming events and planning meetings. 'We could do this', 'we could, but we could also do that', 'yes, but we could also do another thing'. In real terms, three different ideas.

If we swap the word 'but' to the word 'and' we get a very different conversation and outcome. The word 'and' is figuratively a joining word and builds on the idea. Let's go back to the original idea of the friends and substitute the word 'but' with 'and'.

> *Hey, we could go into town tonight, grab a few drinks and have dinner at the Italian.*
>
> Another friend says, *Yeah we could do that and we could also go and see the new movie that has just come out.*

The word 'and' totally changes the story and builds on the first friend's idea and seems like they could do all of it, drinks, dinner and the movie, not one or the other.

When it comes to dealing with objections, we need to utilise the word 'and' instead of 'but'. If the customer hits with a 'yes, but …' and is waiting for the seller to retort with a 'yes, but …' you are both 'butting heads' – yes pun intended. In this scenario, even if the seller beats the customer into submission, the customer will still not buy. They will probably agree to the statement to keep the peace, or more likely something like, 'OK, let me go away and think some more then' and you won't see them again.

Objection-handling acronyms

Below is a compilation of various objection-handling acronyms and you can see many of them follow a similar pattern:

ARC = Acknowledge, Respond, Counter
LAARC = Listen Acknowledge, Access, Respond, Confirm
LAIR = Listen, Acknowledge, Identify Objection, Reverse It
LACE = Listen, Accept, Commit, Explicit Action
FFF = Feel, Felt, Found

Three-step approach to objections

Step 1: Pace the customer by acknowledging the objection.
Step 2: Respond to the objection.
Step 3: Counter question to enable the customer to move on.

Pacing the customer by acknowledging the objection

The customer wants to know that they have been heard so acknowledging their objection is the first thing to do. How you acknowledge, and the wording used, is going to be very important. Accepting that the customer is in a heightened state, ready to be 'butting' heads, you will need to remove this defence mechanism if you are going to be able to engage their rational mind and influence them.

While acknowledging the objection it is important to ensure that you maintain, or regain, rapport by matching and mirroring. This will help the customer stay with you, especially if they feel like they have broken rapport. Playing back what you heard, and seemingly agreeing with your customer will demonstrate empathy, reduce the barrier and keep rapport.

Objection	*Yes but the software seems quite complicated to use.*
Seller	*Yes and I totally understand that it looks complicated, especially on the first time of using it.*

Adding the word 'and' will lower their guard slightly and remove some of the tension in the amygdala (fight or flight) thus starting to provide access to the frontal cortex of the brain where the thinking will really take place.

Sometimes, after acknowledging the objection, further investigation is needed to uncover the true objection. The initial objection could easily be a mask to something else that has not yet been said or is sitting in the back of the customer's mind. Probing in to the objection will help you identify the cause, or the intent, behind the objection. An example response would be, 'OK, I hear what you're saying, and can you help me understand more about that?'

Depending on the strength of the objection and where you believe the customer is in the buying cycle, a trial close prior to answering the objection can work quite well in this situation. For example, using the example above and trial close would be, 'If we can resolve this training issue, would we be in a position to go ahead?'. This type of question acknowledges the customer's objection and ascertains whether there is something else behind the objection. If the customer is reluctant to commit, you know that there is something else to uncover and discover and probe further into the true reason behind the objection.

Responding to the objection

One of the objection acronyms was FFF, or Feel, Felt, Found, which I first read in Zig Ziglar's book, *Secrets of Closing the Sale.*

This technique involves acknowledging the customer's objection by

- empathising with them – 'I understand how you feel'
- sharing a similar experience or story – 'Many of our customers have felt the same way'; and
- sharing a positive outcome or resolution – 'What they found was ...'

This technique is commonly used in sales and customer service contexts because it allows the salesperson or customer service representative to acknowledge the customer's objection, show empathy and understanding, and then provide a positive solution or outcome.

With the Feel, Felt, Found method, people tend to utilise the first of the two Fs in the acknowledge phase, before moving into the response with 'found' statement to overcome the objection.

Customer: *The other software provider offers comprehensive training on their system.*

Seller: *'totally understand why you* ***feel*** *that is a good option. Other customers* ***felt*** *the same way when comparing providers, and what they* ***found*** *was that even when we offered training, our system is so intuitive, the staff and users didn't want or need it.*

Having demonstrated empathy, while maintaining rapport, this should put the customer's mind into a more receptive mode. The response to the objection is now going to be more readily received and hopefully accepted by the customer.

If you have done the right discovery and exploration at the beginning of the sale you should be in a position now to bring back the needs and benefit statements of why you are offering this solution and how it is linked to their own requirements. Solving the solution their way, not yours.

Utilising the power of three, and the solution heartbeat model, you can cap off the end of the response by playing everything back to the customer. Taking the example above it could sound like:

I totally understand why you feel like that, other customers felt the same way, and what they found was our system is so intuitive, the staff and users didn't want or need any training. Like you said previously, having a simple-to-use system was crucial in driving user adoption, reducing roll-out time, and delivering a strong return on investment for the project.

Reframing

Reframing is also a great way of helping customers to see past the obstacle in their mind. Sticking with the software sales example, we can help the customer reframe the situation by borrowing a different example but something very similar.

Customer: Yes but the competitor does offer comprehensive training.
Seller: Interesting, how much training do you currently provide your users on how to use the internet and web browsers like Chrome or Safari?'

Customer: Internet browser? No, everyone knows how to use the browser.
Seller: So since our system is web based, they already know how to use it. Would you prefer a system that is intuitive and easily adopted,

or one that needs a complete training suite to help the users learn how to use it?

This type of repositioning the mindset of the customer helps them come to terms with both strengths of your product and differentiates your value proposition from the competitors.

Counter question to enable the customer to move forward

The final stage is to help the customer move past the objection by asking them to confirm that they are satisfied with the situation. From a psychological perspective it is important for their brain to confirm it is satisfied otherwise something in the subconscious will hold back from committing to the deal. The key here is to get the customer to say yes.

The counter question at the end of the response is as easy as asking the customer a question like *'so can you see why I haven't included a fee for training?'.*

This counter question is utilising the brain operating system (Visual, Audio, Physical) and is asking the question to allow the brain to move forward. In this instance it has used a visual use, i.e. *see why.* Using a visual operating system will mean that the customer will use the imagery of the response and their mind will then take the solution further than what the seller has said. It would not be surprising if the customer continues to talk and open up with additional information and mitigating their own objection.

While we are on the topic of brain operating systems, Feel, Felt, Found as an objection framework is obviously a physical type of response. If you know which operating system your customer is using then modify the FFF to the other option.

Visual:	*I see what you mean,* *other customers saw it the same way, and* *what they have seen ...*
Counter question:	*Can you see why ...?*
Audio:	*I hear what you are saying* *Other customers said the same thing* *And what they have said afterwards ...*
Counter question:	*So does that sound like the ...?*

Physical:	*I understand why you feel like that* *Other customers felt the same way* *And what they found is*
Counter question:	*Knowing that, do you feel this …?*

What happens to personality when it moves into negotiation?

Earlier in the book we looked at Salecology colours to understand personality and how it works in both buyers and sellers. One of the interesting factors of personality is how to reacts to different situations when it is put under pressure.

There is an old saying, 'a little bit of stress in your life is good for you'. I am not sure if anyone who says this has experienced stress. It is a horrible, dark place, which I do not wish on anybody and is not somewhere which is good for you. I believe what they really mean is that people need to be taken out of their comfort zone and stretched a little. The gap between comfort zone and stress (stretch) depends a lot on the person's nature and how familiar they are with stepping out of their comfort zone. Some people love trying new things and experiences, while others love following a well-trodden path. In personal growth and development books, such as *The Art of Possibility*, by Rosamund and Benjamin Zander, they share how it can help individuals overcome their fears and limitations by pushing themselves outside of their comfort zone.

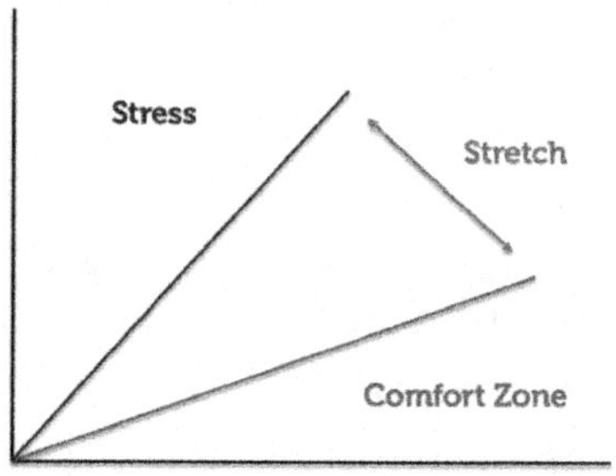

What is interesting therefore is what happens to personality when it moves into the stretch zone. Rather than change personality you will see that their personality colour, or traits, get accentuated and drawn on to deal with the given situation.

Colour personality	Key words	In stretch
Orange energy	• Fun • Social • Creative • Interactive	• More brainstorming • More collaborative • More energy • More creative
Red energy	• Bold • Efficient • Direct • Assertive	• More focused • More action • More directing • More pace
Green energy	• Considerate • Supporting • Harmonious • Reliable	• More personal • More supporting • More hours • More caring
Blue energy	• Factual • Diligent • Structured • Logical	• More detail • More analysis • More planning • More structure

As we know, the Reds are bold, efficient, focused, fast and very action-orientated already. When under pressure they become even more focused, more action-orientated and more direct! You will see them take on a commanding role and start being more assertive in the approach and being quite direct, even blunt, to those around them.

The Oranges are very interactive, fun, sociable, friendly and creative. When they are under pressure, they want to be even more creative, and start to do more brainstorming and collaboration with others to get more interaction and engagement. Thus, drawing on that extraverted energy to help them push forward and manage the situation.

The Greens are very considerate, supportive, sharing and caring individuals. As they feel the pressure, they become even more personal and considerate and start talking more about you with you to ensure you are OK. They are already hard-working but as the pressure mounts, they will put in even more hours to focus on the task in hand while they become even more available and supportive to others.

The Blues, being very factual, diligent, objective, and consistent, when they become under pressure they will require more detail, more analysis and even more structure and planning to feel safe and in control. This increase in knowledge and control will help them strategise and structure a way to achieve the objectives in a consistent and coordinated manner.

Understanding the impact of pressure therefore also refutes another old saying, 'when the going gets tough the tough get going'. Because when the going gets tough we just accentuate our personality and behaviours, and it just means people rise to the occasion in their own way.

Win/Win – I don't think so!

Everyone assumes that the art of negotiation is to find a win-win scenario, but it is not always the outcome people are focused on. One of the aspects of negotiation and bargaining, is to know that there is a psychological current underneath, and personalities can take one of two turns:

1. I become Problem Solver – I will look for a fair deal (win-win).
2. I become Adversarial – my job is to maximise the gain.

One prominent figure in the study of negotiation is Roger Fisher, who co-authored the book *Getting to Yes: Negotiating Agreement Without Giving In* with William Ury and Bruce Patton. In this book, Fisher and his co-authors discuss the importance of adopting a problem-solving approach to negotiation, in which parties work collaboratively to identify common interests and find mutually beneficial solutions. This approach stands in contrast to an adversarial stance, in which parties are in competition with one another and focus on maximising their own outcomes at the expense of the other party.

The problem solver stance

The problem solver stance is the easy one to recognise as it is often the one adopted by the person looking to make a fair deal. Their brain is wired to look for ways for the parties to work together and come to a mutually acceptable agreement.

Cognitively, the problem solver utilises the rational part of the brain and is committed to search for a fair deal. The brain looks to gain knowledge to establish everyone's interests and searches for underlying needs. It is programmed to think 'what can we do to help everyone' as it searches for a solution for all parties. The brain is very flexible and creative in its approach to do this as it is focused and interested in finding that win-win situation.

From a style perspective, you will see the problem solver take a creative approach as they will be open and interested in any abstract idea to find a solution, so nothing is off the table. They have a strong belief that this will be found if everyone is prepared to compromise. During the negotiation they will take a less formal approach and don't engage in the idea of reciprocal (give-and-take) concessions. For them it is about understanding the general concerns and getting everyone on the same page, rather than being drawn into specifics.

The focus of the problem solver is often on maintaining the relationship and looking for mutual gain for both sides. One of the downfalls of this approach can be that the problem solver is so interested in mutual agreement that they can sometimes be taken advantage of and give too much concession.

The adversarial stance

The adversarial stance is more of the role we tend to see when people become those tough negotiators. Their mindset is looking to maximise their gain and is more combative and sees the negotiation as a game to win, or at least get the best deal.

From a cognitive nature the adversarial role is much more structured and planned. The brain considers that knowledge is power and therefore, unlike the problem solver, will be reluctant to share it until they can use it for its advantage. Keeping their card close to their chest, the adversarial looks for data and knowledge to induce, persuade or deceive, in order to win. The brain considers that negotiation is about winners and losers and sets about to ensure it positions itself for the best possible outcome.

Where the problem solver style is creative and flexible in their approach, the adversarial is far more structured and linear, almost one-dimensional.

They are good at articulating and justifying their position, using the facts and data, and have a tendency to be well prepared. Yes, it may create conflict, but they see this as part of the process. The take a route of a) what has been done and agreed, and b) what still needs to be done, and they are strongly focused on a settlement zone.

The challenge with this style is that it lacks empathy and can create long-term damage on the relationship, especially if the losing party feels they have been treated harshly or unfairly. Apart from a friendly bit of haggling for a used car, this approach can often end in a stalemate, where both parties get stuck and no deal is forthcoming, especially when neither party is willing to back down.

Colour stances

Back to our personality colours, it could seem obvious that a combative style is more likely from which colour? – Red, right? Well, yes, it is quite possible that Red will take a more adversarial stance with the idea of dominating the deal and the outward visible competitive nature of the energy. What is interesting is that we could easily think many customers go Red when they go into negotiation, but when we look at the personality colours more closely, we see is that each Salecology colour can be adversarial or problem solver, depending on the situation and the circumstances.

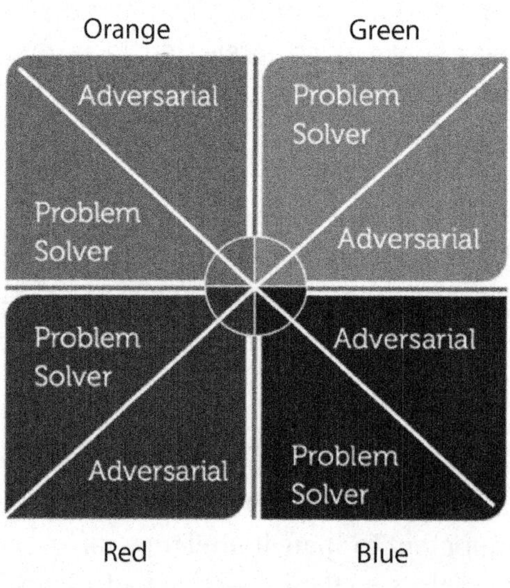

Let's take Green. On the face of it we see harmony and a supportive nature. As they get pulled into a negotiation, and the pressure is turned up, they can be much more collaborative in style, with a win-win mentality. However, if they have a lot of blue colour energy in them being more matter of fact, they may tend to be more adversarial by nature. If not adversarial by nature, this adversarial stance could be triggered if someone seems to be treating them unfairly, and they feel that someone has gone against their moral code or values or acted unethically. They don't however become Red in this context. What you will see is that Green will become more passive aggressive, stubborn, dig their heels in and become uncompromising.

Equally the Red, we would think would be more focused, direct and competitive, seeking to maximise the deal, but should they also have a lot of Orange in them, that intuitive nature, that extraversion can induce a problem solver mode where they still take the lead, but are more open with the information and create some honest open dialogue like 'I know everyone has to get something out of this, and we need to get a good deal, but we want a long-term relationship where we all make money – what can we do to get this closed off?' or 'I don't mind you making money, but I need to get a good deal as well', so they are very open and direct about it.

Moving negotiations to be collaborative

Due to the creation of conflict, the adversarial stance can end in stalemate, can ruin a relationship and there are winners and losers, so one person could end up feeling exploited. The better option therefore is to move the customer away from this adversarial stance into a problem solver mindset. This means they will be more empathetic to the situation and work together to resolve the conflict.

Provide the illusion of control

An important aspect for those that take this adversarial stance is the idea of winning and being in control. We need to help the customer see they are winning, or at least give them the illusion of being in control and winning.

Get the no!

Jim Camp in his 2002 book, *Start with No*, is a great example of how to utilise the word 'no' to give the other person the feeling of being in control. So far in this book, we have obviously focused on how to get the customer to say 'yes' to you, but from a reverse psychology perspective sometimes we need them to say 'no' to get them to say 'yes'. Let me explain more.

We have all been taught to focus on *yes*, gain agreement, and *no* simply means rejection. But in reality, *no* could be an indicator of where the person's mind is and what they are thinking. Camp's philosophy is that *no* can also mean that people are not convinced, or want to exercise their power to preserve their right to say *no*, i.e. be in control. He shares that allowing people to say *no* actually lowers their emotions, gives them the sense of control and therefore opens them up to be more rational. This leads them to be more collaborative when they feel you are not trying to push or persuade them round to your idea. Any techniques trying to push a *yes* onto them, could drive anger and resentment.

By getting the customer to say *no*, we can open them up to what they do and don't want. Understanding when they say *no*, we can put them at ease, and give them the feeling of controlling the situation. Sometimes mislabelling the objection will enable the customer to say *no* and then give you more information about why.

Seller: *So are you saying that you don't want to drive the changes across the business?*
Customer: *No, it's not that, it is just that …*

Whatever comes next will help you identify what they are concerned about fixing that will enable the deal to come together. Getting the customer to say *no* can also be used to influence and/or reframe their thought. Playing back the pains and negative impacts that you uncovered during the initial part of the sale (4Q questions in earlier chapter) can be brought forward here and get them to reinforce the need to change and get the customer to say *no*, while being in control.

You said previously that you need to change the flooring because the tiles are cracked, not only does it look unpleasant, it's difficult to keep clean, but most importantly it's creating danger to those who walk on them. Are you prepared to leave it until some actually falls over?

Find the what

Chris Vos and Tahl Raz, in their 2016 book *Never Split the Difference*, discuss how the FBI engage hostage takers through questioning techniques to give the illusion that they are calling the shots while the negotiator influences their mind. In this aspect they would ask questions to engage the hostage taker into a dialogue and force them to think rather than simply make demands. They named these types of questions 'calibrated questions' as they were calibrated to illicit a certain type of response and build empathy.

The same rules apply when negotiating with a customer who has taken an adversarial mindset. You will need to calibrate your questions to move the customer to be more empathetic to you and slowly move them into a problem solver mindset. Once in the problem solver state you will be able to work together and come to a mutually acceptable outcome.

When considering the questions to ask, be careful. Closed questions, looking for one-word answers, ignites the fight-or-flight response in the other person as they will feel you are trying to persuade them or back them into a corner.

Some open questions also aren't too helpful, in particular the why-type question. We were often asked why questions as children by our parents when we were in trouble for doing something wrong. Why did you do that? Why haven't you done your homework? Why are you late home? and so on. As adults, when we are asked a why question we immediately feel like we need to justify our actions. In this sense, asking someone a why question will in essence reinforce their opinion. Why questions therefore can be useful if we want to take someone back to a positive place and act as a reinforcement. For example, if you are negotiating the renewal of a contract, you could ask a question like, 'you have been a customer for three years now, why did you pick us all those years ago?' The response from this question will reinforce the reasons they chose you in the first place and move them to a happier place.

So which questions should you use? To engage the customer into a dialogue and understand what they are thinking, why they are thinking it, you need to move them into a more rational mindset, rather than the emotional one, where often the drivers for the adversarial position sit (that inner drive to win). Utilising 'what and how' questions will force the customer's brain to engage.

'What' questions are great to explore and uncover aspects of the deal the customer is unhappy or uncertain about. The key here is to engage the customer in dialogue and hopefully get to level 2 in our active listening (a well-reasoned response). Make your questions strong enough that they must think. Some example questions:

What is it about this deal that you feel is not right?
What part of this offer do you feel like I am treating you unfairly?
What did you have in mind?
What can we do to resolve this?

Remember the what type questions are designed to give your customer the feeling of control. There is nothing aggressive in these questions and by asking them in this type of manner, will provide insight into both the rational and emotional mind of the customer.

Ask for help

'How' questions are extremely powerful. Taking a step back for a moment, one of the biggest developers of empathy and forming relationships is asking for help. Asking for help shows vulnerability, encourages understanding, builds trust in others, and fosters reciprocity.

When we ask for help, in essence we are admitting that we don't have all the answers and we need the assistance of others. This vulnerability can create a bond between people and makes us more relatable to others. Equally, by asking for the help, we are showing trust in the person we are asking to provide us with assistance, which can also create a deeper connection and build a stronger relationship.

Moreover, by asking for help, you are demonstrating that you value the other person's expertise or knowledge, and this can be a compliment to them. This can lead to a greater sense of mutual respect and understanding, and help to foster empathy between you.

How questions ask the other person for help. They can show the things just stated above, reduce the defensiveness in your customer, and start to use their mental and emotional capacity to work with you to overcome the challenges. Hence now in a more problem solver mindset. Some example how questions:

> *How can we resolve this?*
> *How can we solve this situation together?*
> *How do you expect me to be able to do that?*
> *How can we move this forward?*

Build empathy before the negotiation!

An interesting study conducted by Michael Morris, from Stanford University, pitted two groups of MBA students against one another to ascertain the role of rapport and relationships in invoking better outcomes, especially when working in a remote negotiation setting. This is interesting in today's world where negotiations are not always face to face but can take place on email, message services or video call – where often the camera ends up being turned off! What Morris found was that sharing something personal on the call or email prior to the negotiation delivered a significant impact on people and they tended to take a more collaborative approach rather than adversarial.

Of course, having rapport and humanising the deal before going into the negotiation is going to be extremely helpful and some procurement people try their best to dehumanise it, and make it more about price and availability. Remember that although they try and put on this persona, they are human and still have emotions and often will pick a colour stance, and either an adversarial or problem solver position. Humanising the conversation will have a huge impact on this conversation. In the next few pages, we look at how to use some psychological aspects in framing and dealing with price.

Dealing with price

Price concerns

Objections based on price are the most common that salespeople share with me. Price objections are the easiest excuse for a customer to give to a seller if they are choosing a competitor – why? Because the salesperson feels like they have a good excuse to play back to their manager about why the customer didn't buy. That said, it is not fair to simply blame the seller either; sometimes the customer loses sight themselves of what they are buying and the long-term benefits of the product or solution.

As we saw at the beginning of the chapter, selling on features alone will drive a price objection as the buyer considers the value of features does not equal the cost. The clue here is to understand value instead of price. If you haven't uncovered value and benefits, then it is time to go back to your questioning skills to uncover the value before dealing with the price objection.

The first rule when getting into price is to understand how your product and services are priced. Depending on the type of products and services you sell, it could be cost plus model, going rate (market rate), tiered subscription, premium pricing, or a value-based model to name a few. Understanding how the product price is ascertained will make it easier for you to speak to the customer about why the price is the price.

The person you are selling to, when it comes towards the end of the sell, will often try to view your product as a commodity model, e.g. I am comparing your price with all the other potential vendors for my needs. Your job is to help them get back into understanding value instead of price.

Ask questions to understand and confirm their rationale behind the objection, who is most troubled, how and what are they comparing against the competitor. Try and confirm key points of the pricing.

Having probed into the source of the price concern, different things may come to light; it could be scepticism, a misunderstanding, a real concern, or a serious potential drawback. This will allow you to address the objection directly and/or utilise the ARC model to demonstrate the value of the solution as opposed to deal with price.

Framing the price

Looking at pricing at the start of the negotiation is an interesting start point. Firstly, if you price ends in a 0 or 99, it can signal to the customer that the price has been made up rather than calculated. If the price is £1,000 or £999, does that sound like an arbitrary price or do you believe the seller has calculated the exact price? People have started to become a little immune to certain numbers, e.g. if someone says I'll be two mins, do we believe they will be two mins exactly or they won't be much longer, what about five mins, or ten mins? What if someone said I'm three minutes away, or I'll arrive in seven minutes – we will think this is a precise number and expect them in three or seven minutes.

The same works on pricing. If the price is an odd number, not ending in 0s or 5s or 9s, people believe it to have been calculated and find the price more believable and genuine. For example, if the project renovation quotations for your home came in at £23,764 does that sound more genuine than the quotation that says it is £23,750.

Typical buyer tricks

Look at these ten buyer tactics and tick off the ones you might have seen, heard or even used yourself!

Name	Usage example	√
Shock	'How much? – you must be joking! – you should be wearing a mask that's day-light robbery.'	
Strike first	'I am happy to order … if we can agree a 10% discount.'	
Meet me halfway	'Let's split the difference.'	
Competitor threat	'You are much more expensive than your competition.'	

Budget	'It's all we can afford'/'I only have this in the budget.'
Broken record	Keep repeating the request for the price and eventually the salesperson will buckle.
Economic buyer	'If we can agree a 20% discount then I can get the board/CFO/my boss to sign it off.'
Silence	Use silence – don't be used by it.
Personal favour	'I have gone a long way to get this signed off internally, I just need you to give me this special rate, can you help me out?'
Double down	Negotiate hard on a single year, then ask for a multi-year term.
Deliberate misunderstanding	'I thought it included …'

Suspending belief

What do you believe the margin or mark-up is on a new car from the dealership? How about the margin on a new kitchen? What percentage do you think the software company makes on your user licences? The truth is everyone has a belief on how much money the company is making out of the deal, whether that belief is true or not. This belief will direct the negotiator on where they expect to do the deal, i.e. their settlement zone. To maintain the margin and give the customer a sense of winning, you need to reframe their mind in terms of where the best deal sits.

Open with the full price

The important aspect of any deal is to show the customer what is the full price. Many salespeople seem to tell the customer a price after discount. The problem here is that the customer will want to barter on the price you have given and mentally has skipped the initial discount they have received.

For example, a carpet retailer has a sale with a 30% discount and therefore advertises the price as mark down from \$20 to £14 per m^2. The customer needs $20m^2$.

The typical salesperson will do the simple calculation and tell the customer it is \$280 for the carpet. The customer is now price conditioned that the price is \$280 and will start to bargain from that point.

If the seller had told the customer that it comes to \$20 x $20m^2$ = \$400, but due to the special discount rate they receive \$120 off today and will only have to pay \$280, this price conditions the customer at \$400 and gets them to see that they have already received a bargain. For many customers this will be more than enough, but some will still want to feel like they have maxed out the discount and will engage in some of the tactics explored above.

Give not take

The second rule in dealing with price is that it is better to give than take. If I give you something worth \$40, is it the same as giving you a discount of \$40? Well, it depends – the item I give you for \$40 would be the retail value not the cost price, however if I give you \$40 discount that is costing \$40 of profit. To the customer they both have equal value, to the company one is a lot more expensive than the other.

'Give' in this instance means giving something extra, it doesn't mean start including items for free that the customer wants to buy, otherwise you are simply giving away margin. The idea is that you use give and take once you have come to the price of the deal, the money remains the same, but you are using a give rather than a discount.

Talk money not percentages

People don't understand percentages in a negotiation and therefore if you fall into the trap of talking about percentages in a discount strategy the customer will always not equate that to real money. For example, if I said you get 2.2% discount you would be thinking I haven't even tried and am not interested in winning the deal. By talking about money instead of percentages the customer will understand and value the saving more.

Reframing the margin

Sometimes you will need to give concessions on price as part of the bargaining process. This is where you will need to reframe their mind on how much margin and discount is available. A simple rule of thumb is whatever concession you give, cannot be repeated at the same value. Let me show you how this works:

Seller	Buyer
The price is $1,000 but with today's special discount it comes to $850.	The buyer starts to haggle on the price *utilising some of the tactics listed above *'how much, you must be joking, I'll give you $500'*
	The customer presumes there is a large margin to negotiate with.
As you can see, we have already discounted the price by $150, I can probably go an extra $20, that's $170 off	*Only $20, I'll tell you what, let's split the difference, you at $830, and I'm at $500, let's call it $650.*

This small discount reframes the customer's mind, as he is expecting the price to come down in $100s not such a short amount.

Seller	Buyer
I wish I could, but you have already beaten the price point, I can go another $5 if that helps you.	*Oh, OK, well I think we can probably go ahead with that, does it include anything else?*

This reduction in the further concession indicates to the customer's subconscious that the amount of discount available has probably been reached.

The primary focus is always on moving the customer back to value and not price. Of course, you can replay the heartbeat or benefit statements, which is a good option, however, the customer might need to sell it a little more to themselves. A question such as:

If the product performs the way we have discussed, would the value of it outweigh the cost?

Part 3 – Building your Emotionally Intelligent Sales Organisation

This book has explained quite a lot of different ways of utilising facets of psychology to influence outcomes. With the right training and environment, you can develop people's emotional intelligence, but wouldn't it be better to ensure you hire the right people in the roles that can fast track that aspect?

A question often asked of us at Salecology is: 'are salespeople born or made?' The truth is both – not helpful I know. There are certain aspects of selling that come naturally to some, and others need to learn. It is of course those natural talents that shine through with the early career salespeople or those that fast track their career and take to it like a duck to water. That said,

Experience is not the predictor of future performance

Having worked with many organisations to help map and define 'what good looks like' from their people, there are various behavioural sciences that help identify those aspects which can be strong predictors of future success in people within your organisation. Shockingly, experience is not the answer. When we cross-examined the various attributes of those who are successful in transforming to the new world, what became clear is that just because someone has two years, or ten years' experience in the field, doesn't mean that they will be successful in the new organisation or new role. Of course, it is useful that someone understands the market, the language and technical jargon, but this is not a predictor of success.

Right at the beginning of this book, we looked at the different eras of selling, and when you understand people's sales tenure, you can see

that type of sales behaviour in them. For example, selling ten years in the tech space, and joining a new organisation, doesn't tell you how quickly the new person will be able to get up to speed with the new products and services, selling with the new methodology or moving into selling in a tougher economic environment; the past performance ceases to be the important aspects.

Having the right people, doing the right things, accelerates sales performance. Many organisations expend huge resources determining their product and market strategies but fail to assess whether their people can make the transition to the new approach – so growth is stifled by the sales force itself.

All too often, the top 20% of salespeople make up 80% of revenue. The challenge for an organisation is to identify the characteristics and behaviours that separate the top performers from the rest, and then to replicate those characteristics across the group.

The three core elements of building a sales organisation are:

The right people –	having the right aptitude, personality, motivations, capability and behaviour
Doing the right things –	with the right knowledge, skills, behaviour and strategy
Delivering the results –	who are being coached and led to deliver the right output

This part of the book looks at how to implement a more emotionally intelligent sales structure and model. How to assess, select and recruit the right aptitude, how to build your sales approach and methodology, and how to coach and embed a high-performance mindset into your team.

Have I got the right salespeople?

One of the consistent problems with recruitment is that managers tend to assess candidates based on the wrong criteria – namely experience and capability. Although these aspects are interesting, research shows that they are not actually good predictive indicators of a salesperson's ability to be a top performer within another organisation and culture. By knowing what 'good and great' looks like, and utilising assessment tools, enables your recruiters to conduct more in-depth, objective screening and will ensure you always hire the right people for the right roles. Getting this right has a huge impact on creating high performance and ensuring new recruits start contributing earlier.

What does great look like in your organisation?

Defining what good/great looks like should allow you to define the type of individual who will succeed in your given role, contextual to your company culture, ambition and marketplace. If you have ever hired a 'top performer' from a competitor, you will know that a great salesperson in one company doesn't always fit into another!

Utilising a more scientific and psychological approach to identifying and selecting talented individuals will ensure those selected will have what it takes to quickly become high performers. I mentioned earlier that experience is a low predictor of performance so what is? Measuring aptitude, personality, motivations and behaviours you can create a 'What Great Looks Like profile', which from experience will triple hiring accuracy and identify which people can, and will, succeed in the role in your organisation. You can also utilise it to pinpoint developmental needs and build targeted behavioural programmes. It also means that you will be able to accurately measure the impact and results both on behavioural change and performance.

Aptitude

Aptitude is a combination of a person's intellectual faculty and their ability to learn, take in, process and retain information. Does the person have the natural ability to understand both written and verbal information, can they read between the lines and understand what is and isn't being said? Can they interpret what the numbers are telling them and make the right decisions, or ask the right questions from them? Emotional intelligence can also be included in the aptitude assessment. For example, can the person spot and interpret people's emotions correctly, and make the right inferences based on thoughts and feelings.

In short, if someone has the skills to learn quickly and take in the information provided, they can quickly learn in months what experienced people took years to learn.

Ability tests are great for assessing aptitude. Utilise some of those listed below:

Verbal reasoning	This test measures the ability to make correct decisions or inferences from verbal data. The emphasis in these tasks focus on understanding and evaluating written information and applying critical thinking to it.
Numerical reasoning	Like verbal reasoning, this measures the ability to make correct decisions or inferences from numerical data. The emphasis in these tasks is on understanding and evaluating data rather than on computation.
Diagrammatic	Diagrammatic reasoning measures the ability to see patterns and linkages within data provided.

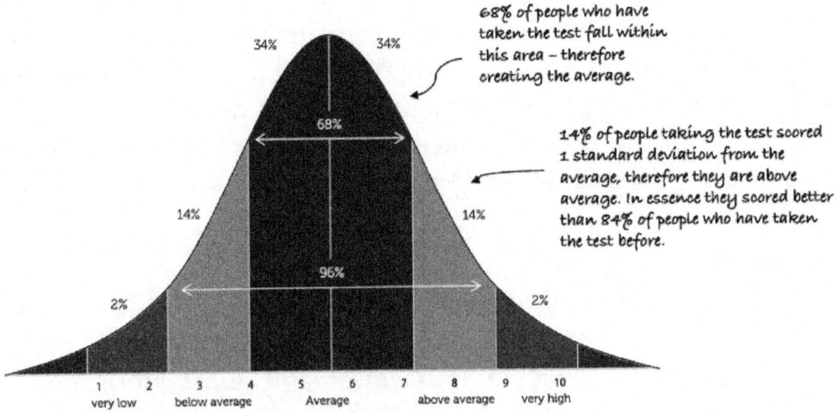

The way people are measured in these tests are against a norming group. A norming group is a representation of those who have taken the test before and the score for the candidate is benchmarked against this group to determine how they scored compared to that audience of their peers.

The norming group scores are plotted on a bell curve, using standard deviation, so you can see the distribution of marks and determine where the potential recruit scores. In essence, what you are really interested in is whether the person is below, average or above average against a group of peers. Depending on your customer base, market and product complexity, and role requirement you can determine what is the best fit for the role.

Personality

The person's personality is something that will demonstrate cultural fit into the organisations and also the style in which they will interact with others. Personality effects the way we interact, influence, take decisions and our approach to different aspects of the sale. Understanding the personalities, similarities and differences, allows us to accurately predict behaviour and performance. We already looked deeply into personality earlier in the book and the various aspects of it. Personality helps identify how people will act in certain situations and which parts of the sales cycle they have a natural affinity towards, and which parts they may shy away from. Personality will also identify aspects like sales style, resilience, decision-making style, social confidence, levels of independence and so on.

When looking to utilise psychometric testing in selection be very careful to only use it in conjunction with other tools and the interviews. You should never make decisions using psychometrics on their own. Also note there are two different theories of psychometrics, trait and type theory. One of the widely known type psychometrics is the Myers Briggs Type Indicator (the clue is in the name) and Raymond Cattell was one of the early pioneers of Trait theory. The easiest way to explain the difference is to consider a 'type' is putting the person into a category – for example they are either introvert or extrovert, whereas trait theorists would plot someone along the line between introversion and extraversion.

In the world of recruitment and selection you are much better off, and according to the world's various psychological societies it is more ethically appropriate, to use trait theory. In this sense you can ascertain how much of a person's character should be the various traits.

For example, on a scale of 1–10 how much extroversion would the ideal candidate need to be more successful in the role or within your business? If they are a 10 is that too much for your customers, will a 1 be too reserved? The thing to do is select a short range – e.g. 7 or 8 but be open to look at 6 or a 9 – depending on the other scores.

	Low			Medium			High			
Extroversion	1	2	3	4	5	6	7	8	9	10

How about resilience on a scale of 1–10. Too resilient and the person might be so laid back that they are not prepared to up the pace when the going gets tough, or you may not see them react to the final push at the end of the quarter. Too little resilience and they might buckle under pressure and become despondent on those tougher months when business isn't going their way. The same as before, select a range and review the people against it.

	Low			Medium			High			
Resilience	1	2	3	4	5	6	7	8	9	10

Looking at the personality factors, map all those personality factors that are important to your business, and look at tools that can help you measure those objectively, from part of the interview process and utilising psychometric tests.

Motivations

Motivations are the things that drive people to do the things they do. It is underpinned by personal values, but also our natural tendencies to move toward or away from things. We always look for and assess people's motivations especially within the sales roles and organisation. We look for intrinsic motivations – the things that people find enjoyable and get satisfaction out of; and extrinsic motivations – the things that are externally motivations such as monetary reward.

The intrinsic motivations are by far more compelling and will be used as the person's moral compass, but also determine which parts of the role they will tend to gravitate towards and which ones to shy away from.

The extrinsic motivations will change with time, without getting started on Maslow's hierarchy of needs, typically early career people are motivated by money initially, but those who are more successful might be something else. We have also seen a huge difference between generations and motivations for those Baby Boomers, Gen X, Millennials and now Gen Z. Gen Z today are more willing to work for an organisation that has higher growth opportunities and more entrepreneurial, whereas the Millennials were more into the fun office stuff like ping-pong tables and the bring-your-dog-to-work policy.

Understanding what motivations and values the person has will enable you to determine whether they can succeed, enjoy and flourish in the environment they will be working in.

So how do you uncover motivations:

Motivation questionnaires	There are psychometric questionnaires that can be used to ask a range of questions that identify what motivates you at work. It can be either generic, specific to a particular role, or look at aspects of work such as Understanding and Implementing; Working within Systems; Teamworking and Communicating.
Personality profiles	As seen previously, personality profiles can also be useful to look at cognitive behaviour and understand how people like to be recognised, perceived and rewarded, and what aspects motivate them.
121 interview	Obviously in a 121 interview you can ask questions to seek out things that they hold near and dear to their heart, what aspects they share with you, things they feel are important. Be careful to dig into this as they

	may not know what they strive for as this is often a subconscious and emotional driver.

Capability

Capability is a combination of knowledge, skill and behaviour. The most important one of these is behaviour. When interviewing or reviewing people, look for 'what people do' rather than 'what can they do'. If someone that has been in sales for any amount of time, there is a good chance that they can talk a good game and could easily share with you some knowledge of what sales is about and what needs to be done to make the sale. They may have attended several training courses as well so can share some nice phrases and terminology. None of this tells you what they do in the moment, and although they know what to do – can they, and are they, able to do it? What people do, as seen earlier, is brought about by aptitude, personality and motivations, but to dig deeper into if the person can actually do what they say utilises some of the tools below:

Competency-based interview	Competency-based interviews use questions to find out how you have used specific skills in your previous experience and how you approach problems, tasks and challenges. Use behaviour or situational-type questions to ask how people used the skills and/or overcame the challenges.
Behavioural event interview	The focus of a BEI interview is to elicit behavioural events. The interviewee is asked to describe, in detail, the five or six most important situations he or she has experienced in a specific job. The situations should include two or three high points, or major successes, and two or three low points, or key failures. These BEIs are usually used at a more senior level as they can take much longer and are sometimes recorded so they can be analysed for evidence of competency.

Assessment centres	A selection centre/assessment day, invites several candidates to attend an event where they partake in a number of exercises to assess their suitability and measure them against the behaviours and competencies required. They give the opportunity to assess and differentiate between candidates who seem very similar in terms of quality and on paper, and highlight what people do, rather than what they say.

Experience

Experience is the combination of the person's life and career experiences to date. You can often see this from the CV such as work history, previous roles, tenure, courses attended and so on. This obviously has some benefits – do they know the industry, have some sales experience, know the jargon, etc.? Although this is the lowest level of future performance predictability when combined with the rest of the stack above it adds value and can be used to assess how people have progressed and experienced life and their upbringing, which has brought them to this point in time.

Understanding experience is about:

CV/resumé/profile	The person's resumé will often highlight their career path, roles, education and potentially some hobbies as well.
Social media	Checking people out on their LinkedIn page, and other social media sites, indicate some of the things they like, demonstrates more about hobbies and activities, such as sporting achievements, charitable work and things they 'like'.
Interview	The telephone interview and first meeting can also be used to uncover past work experience, life experiences where people can provide some colour to their life and world, and allows you to see the world through their eyes. This allows you to screen

the candidates quickly to ensure they meet the requirements of the role.

Assessing talent for the new world

A sales transformation, or reboot, is about identifying whether those people in your organisation can make the transition to the new world. Having been through many sales transformations, you often find yourself putting people into one of three categories: those that you are confident will make it in the new world, those who you are pretty sure won't, and then a number of people in the middle bucket, those you are unsure. This is the same story right across the sales organisation, from the directors and managers through to the team leaders and sales representatives.

Utilising the complete stack, you can define what good looks like today and what will it look like for tomorrow. You can then assess the talent within the business against the profiles to get a much more objective view of those people. Check for two things:

Potential: this is rooted in the intrinsic characteristics of the individual. In particular it takes into account their aptitude, values and motivations.

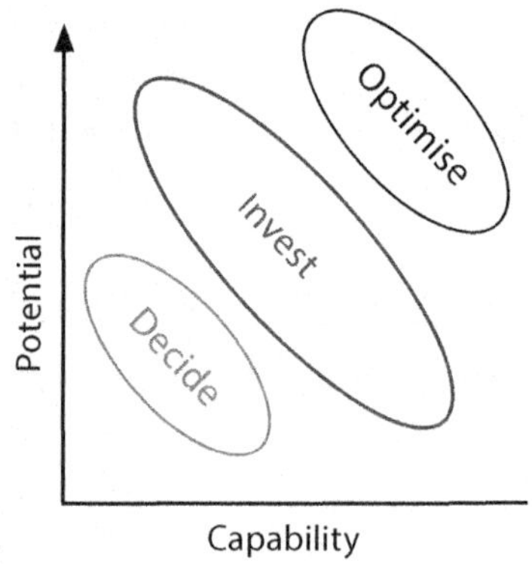

Current capability: this is driven in particular by the behaviours that the individual uses in order to perform their role. We usually assess whether they have all the behaviours required and at what level and with what consistency they use them.

Profiling everyone against the complete stack enables you to split the group into three easily definable groups: **Decide, Invest, Optimise.**

Decide You can find better, we know there is little chance they will turn into the person you need for this role and are not right for the business. They may have expertise you value and have been kept around due to their specialism, but ultimately you will have to end up making a decision.

Invest	There are some real gems in there. Make the best of these people through development and giving them opportunities to grow. Bottom right are the great contributors and performers who might need new clarity on where to go. Top left are often new players with raw potential.
Optimise	These are your A players and the future managers/leaders of the business. They demonstrate a mix of both potential and capability. The development programme for these should be tailored, advanced and potentially based on 121 based coaching.

The same rules apply for promotion, rather than promoting those who seem to be smashing their sales numbers, you can utilise the framework to ascertain if they have the right fit for the role, not just time served and sales success.

How do I build 'our way' of selling?

Having hired and or engaged the right people, you will need to be clear on the various knowledge skills and behaviours the salespeople must have at each part of the process. The skills and behaviours required to engage a customer into the conversation are quite different to the skills required to uncover their needs, which again is different to those needed to demonstrate the value of the product or service and so on.

The earlier chapters in this book define a variety of sales psychology to help the salesperson influence outcomes, but here you need to help the salesperson identify when to pull the various tools out of the bag and lead the customer through the journey.

We have helped many organisations build their 'way of selling'. Sales organisations sometimes make the classic error of deciding how they want to sell, rather than first understanding how customers want to buy.

The customer journey

The customer journey is where sales and marketing come together. By taking time out to look at how the customer goes about buying the solutions you offer will enable you to spot all the various touchpoints you have with them and maximise your opportunity to continue to build trust at each point.

Mapping the journey

This journey mapping can be done to quite a deep level and should look at a number of different touchpoints which start long before they actively engage in shopping around for products. There is a whole passive moment where they may be subconsciously noticing things, or are just frustrated as things are changing in their world and they start to become conscious that they might need to do something about it.

The first step in mapping the journey is to consider:

1. What are they doing?
2. Where are they doing it?
3. What do they want and need?

EQ in the journey

Also as you start thinking about these three steps, you also should make this more emotionally intelligent and add two more pieces to this journey:

4. What are they thinking?
5. How are they feeling?

This reflection provides huge empathy with the customer throughout their journey and provides insight into how to differentiate the touchpoints, build rapport and influence the outcome. I often find working through the 'how are they feeling' part of the customer journey the most enlightening. I was mapping this once for a bespoke kitchen design and manufacturing company and seeing the emotional roller coaster a customer goes through was astonishing. The first stage, unhappy with the current kitchen, moving to intrigue when shopping around and looking at new ones, confusion when presented with the various options, nervous when negotiating, champagne when they ordered, exhausted when needing to make final decisions and final site survey, to despair when their house is turned upside and turned into a building site, to jubilation when it was finished and having friends round. As I said, a complete roller coaster.

Understanding this emotional aspect of the customer journey helps the seller manage the customer in a much better way, demonstrating empathy, but also becoming proactive in minimising the fluctuations of emotions. Also, understanding the emotions enables you to build better sales tools to continue to build confidence in selecting the seller and the organisation throughout the process.

Mapping the sales process

Having defined the customer journey, it becomes easier to wrap the sales process around it. Consider each step the customer goes through and align it to the various stages for your sales process.

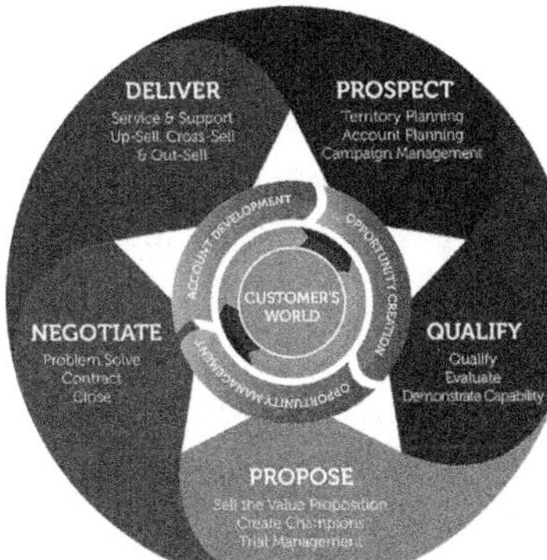

A lot of organisations utilise the default pipeline names provided from their CRM system. Although useful and better than nothing, consider creating your own that are more meaningful for the sales process and customer journey.

The image above demonstrates a typical sales cycle for a software as a service (SaaS) organisation that is wrapped around the customer journey/ buying cycle.

Example process

Below is a breakdown example of how that was mapped.

Prospect – mapping the territory, the accounts within it and building out some sales campaigns.

Qualify – this covers off perhaps a couple of key steps, qualify an opportunity exists, and evaluate whether it is worth pursuing.

For SaaS type organisations the qualify state also includes demonstrating capability and credibility. Similar to the experience of SalesForce.com, as mapped in the book *Predictable Revenue* by Aaron Ross, the prospecting and qualify stage may be owned by a sales development representative (SDR) who warms up opportunities and then hands them across to an account executive (AE) who will take it the rest of the way through the sales cycle. The demonstrate capability/credibility would only encompass a small demo of the product, if at all. Usually, it is demonstrating how the solution would help meet the needs, not an actual product demonstration.

Propose – this stage is where the seller moves into demonstrating the value of the solution and into formal needs and how it matches the customer's criteria. From a Salecology EQ perspective, the seller should also move from selling to their champion, to selling with them into the rest of the organisation.

Negotiate – this part of the sales cycle is about problem solving, objection-handling as well as negotiating the close. It covers off those steps of getting the terms and conditions aligned and getting the deal signed off.

Once the customer has bought, for some organisations, SaaS as the example above, hand over the client to the customer success (CS) team who are focused on getting the customer live on the system and manages the relationship afterwards, including renewals, upswells and potentially cross-selling.

Deliver – is therefore about ensuring the customer is satisfied that the solution delivers on their needs and then moves into selling additional products and services before the contract renewal takes place.

Define the knowledge, skills and behaviours

Having mapped the stages, you can now drill down into deeper aspects required for each of the areas.

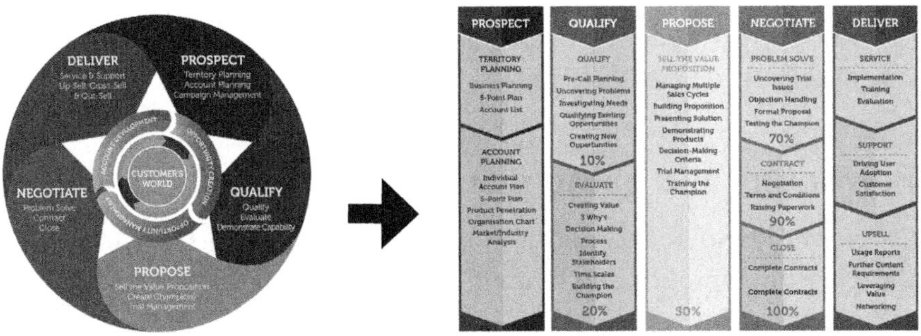

As you can see from the example, each stage then maps the various attributes within it. Each of these will enable you to define the knowledge the salesperson will need to be able to undertake that particular aspect of the sales stage, the skill set required to perform well, and the types of behaviour you would expect to see when they are performing that task.

Let's take one aspect from the example and expand it:

Sales stage: Qualify

Action: Uncovering problems

Knowledge: Product knowledge, industry knowledge (this could be expanded out)

Skill set: Questioning techniques (problem questions, open questions, background questions, etc.)

Behaviour: Explore customer problems during conversations and move away from background questions and drill into customer's issues, challenges and dissatisfaction.

The behaviour aspect of this will migrate back to what was defined in 'what great looks like' discussed in the previous chapter. Be particular about how you would expect to see the behaviour as this will become paramount when you move into coaching in the right behaviour.

Building your methodology

People often talk about sales methodology. To keep it simple, for me methodology is what you have just mapped out. It is the how you do what you do.

What is your method of asking questions? The same goes for what is your method of doing an account review, call plan, opportunity plan and so on. Don't get stuck on the term methodology; remember building 'your way of selling' will be exactly that – your way.

Playbooks and game plans

Once everything is mapped it is easy to start to build out particular strategies to approach different industries, companies or personas.

We have already mapped out for you in Part 2 of this book how to conduct a pain and gain to understand what problems your features solve. To build out a playbook or game plan you need to pull everything together for your salespeople to understand how to apply various techniques and approaches from the models provided in different scenarios.

Before going any further, I want to caveat the next couple of paragraphs by saying that every sales approach should be authentic and unique to the individual customer. The salesperson must read the customer in front of them and set the game play accordingly, the role of the playbook or game plan is to assist in providing them with strategy and structure, not a script!

Building a sales playbook for your team should comprise of some standard aspects as they will be used for new hires as well as your existing sales team.

Company information

The first part of a complete sales playbook should give your new hires a solid overview of your company. Include aspects such as:

- company strategy (and how sales org fits into it)
- mission, vision and values – why the company does what it does
- organisation chart – how the sales teams are structured, plus support functions, and key contacts for various products, etc.

Product value propositions

Utilise this section to provide an overview of your products and services.

- Core messaging and positioning
- Key features and functionality
- Tangible benefits
- Key differentiators

Target personas

A big aspect to consider in your sales playbook is to consider who is the target customer for your product or service. It is important for you to paint a clear picture of your ideal customer profile (ICP) and if selling into businesses, who are the various job titles that could become involved in the buying process.

Below are some aspects to consider when mapping buyer personas:

- Job title
- Role in the decision-making process
- Typical day in the life
- How they are measured (KPIs)
- Typical problems and pain points
- How our product helps solve those problems
- Key messaging

If you are selling to consumers, some other things to consider:

- Demographic
- Lifecycle
- Motivation and goals
- Frustrations
- Buying behaviour

Case examples

Great assets to include in a sales playbook are some real examples of how people have utilised your product and services, the problems they had, how it solved them and the benefits they received.

Pain and gain analysis (PGA)

Utilising the pain and gain analysis discussed in the earlier chapters, take time to map some of the PGA based on the persona.

Sales approach

The playbook will obviously include the sales process and methodology that you have mapped out. In addition to this, consider providing some strong examples of how to run sales plays for the different personas and/or scenarios:

- Key insights to share with the customer
- Sample initial positioning statements (IPSs)
- Main pain points based on the insight
- Problem and impact questions
- Value and Impact questions
- Value propositions to highlight
- Example case studies
- Differentiators and competitors
- Typical objections you may hear
- How to respond

Scripts, templates and cadences

Having mapped the sales plays above, you can take it further and provide some sample call and email scripts to help the new hires understand how to continue their sales cadence and contact strategy with the buyer. Customers can quickly be turned off if they feel you are using a script so special care must be made to coach the team on the dangers of copy and paste, and the use of scripts and templates.

How do I coach for high performance?

Every leader I speak to says for all the sales development work they have instigated into their business, the thing they should have spent more on, both in terms of time and money, was developing the coaching capability of their sales managers. It is the managers and leaders that directly affect the adoption and embedding of the behaviour changes implemented into a team or organisation.

There are four areas of high performance:

1. Know what to do
2. Able to do it
3. Equipped to do it
4. Want to do it

When looking at your organisation, consider these four areas and determine what areas you currently perform well in, and perhaps where you may have a shortfall.

Know what to do

Knowing what to do is a strong concept and not to be underestimated. Challenge yourself and the management team to ensure they know what to do. In the previous chapter we looked at building 'Your way of selling'. It mapped out each of the sales stages, the activities within it and even the knowledge, skills and behaviours expected within it. Do your management team and coaches truly understand the tools and techniques?

Able to do it

Being able to do something is very different to knowing what to do. You may know how a bike works, there are two wheels, a chain is attached to some pedals, when you cycle the pedals round it rotates the back wheel and propels you forward. This doesn't mean that you are able to ride the bike! The same rules apply to sales. You may know that you need to ask questions, you may even know the question types to ask – doesn't mean that you can use them in earnest.

Equipped to do it
This aspect asks the question whether people have the tools and resources necessary to undertake the work. You might know what to do, even able to do it, but just don't have the equipment to do it. I will come back to this in a moment, to look at whether you have built the tools in 'your way of selling' or have the right coaching tools to support embedding behaviour.

Want to do it
The three items above could all be implemented skilfully but if those people you are working with are not mentally and physically engaged, i.e. they don't want to do it, then the first three are redundant. Want is a combination of reward and recognition, linked back to those intrinsic and extrinsic aspects discussed earlier – finding the right people, and identifying the right motivations.

These four aspects not only apply to the sales organisation as a whole but also to the sales manager delivering the coaching. Do they know what to do, are they able to do it, are they equipped to do it and do they want to coach and embed the new behaviour.

The manager must go on the training

The first rule is that the manager must go on the training themselves. This sounds like a silly statement, but I can't tell you how many organisations I have worked with that try to say the managers don't need to attend the workshops, they are too busy, can they just do the coaching workshop. How else will they understand and know the nuances of the new behaviour, understand what the training was about, the inferences made, the right and wrong use of the tools, etc.

That isn't to mean that you should expect the coaches to be the experts in using the sales behaviour. The role of the coach isn't to be the best player, the role of the coach is to be able to spot the behaviour in action and coach people to perform better. If they don't go through the training and content as a delegate, then they cannot remind their sales colleague about the tools from the workshop, will assume they know what it is and will potentially water down the new skill and behaviour when trying to coach it.

Is it a skill or a will issue

The second part of developing your sales team is to identify where the problem lies for the individual; is it that they know what to do but are unable to do it (skill) or is it that they know what they should be doing but they just don't do it (will)?

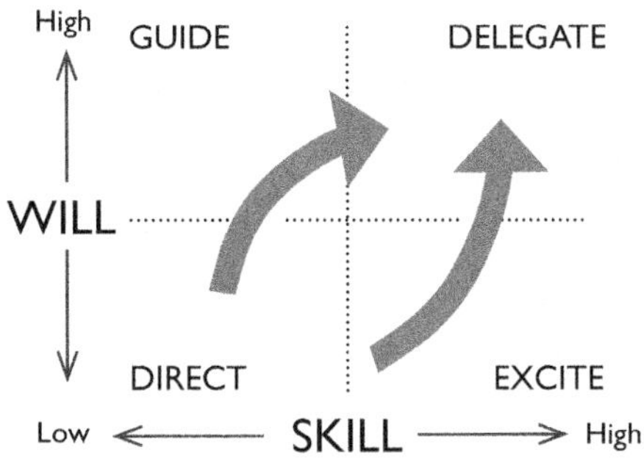

Too often the sales manager/coach reaches for the training button to educate the individual when it is not really a skill issue at all, it is more of a motivational issue. Take a salesperson who has been successful to date, believes they know it all, and therefore doesn't want to adopt these new techniques. Max Landsberg, in his book *The Tao of Coaching*, modelled different behaviours to utilise depending on where people sat on the skill/will matrix.

High will, low skill

When people first start a new job or take on new responsibilities it is usual that you have people who have a high level of willingness to do the work and are open to lots of new ideas. These people are often great to work with as they are striving to be successful. The coaching role for these fit under the title 'guidance'. The coaching style for this will be much more training and teaching, and you will find a person who is very open to receiving it. You will need to provider direction for this person, make sure you create time for weekly check-ins and consider reward and recognition to maintain their high spirits. Also accept they will make some mistakes and learning from those is all part of the process.

High will, high skill

These are your high performers; they have above-average skills and capabilities to deliver the tasks and the motivation to make it happen. There is a tendency to spend more time with this audience because they are fun to be with and the coach themselves learn a lot from them. Of course, you need to nurture this group to ensure they maintain their level of drive and enthusiasm and ensure they don't drop down the Will axis.

From a coaching perspective this should be more of an empowerment move, to enable the person to run with the new behaviours and have additional conversations about where they personally want to evolve and develop. Because of their high will and high skill, these people also tend to look for any new nugget of information that they can add to their repertoire that will enable them to increase performance.

High skill, low will

Sadly, the direction of travel for many people in a workplace can be from high will/low skill, to high skill/high will, and then they slowly become demotivated and drop to high skill/low will. They sort of start jogging along rather than running like they did before.

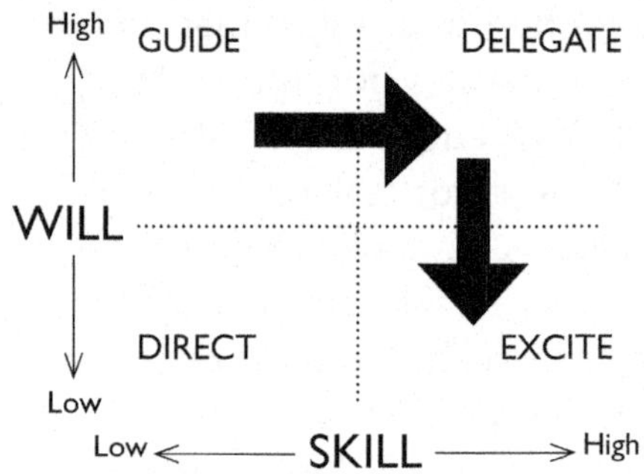

This comes down to the person's engagement and the coach/manager's ability to understand why this is happening. It could be that they are no longer being challenged enough or have just got bored with the role and need some new goals or incentives. The role of the coach here is to excite and motivate the person back into the high will box.

Consider some of the things below:

Job enlargement	also known as horizontal expansion, is about increasing the size of the activities of their role, i.e. bigger area, more product lines, etc.
Job enrichment	also known as vertical expansion, is about giving them more opportunities to do different things, i.e. coach others, host some of the sales meetings, mentoring, etc.
Job rotation	move them into a different department or role for a short period to change their work and focus
Projects	consider putting them into some special projects to excite them back into the work.

As the coach, the important things to do here is to talk openly with the person to uncover what is driving their demotivation. Then digging deeper, you will be able to see what is possible to excite them back into the high will/high skill mindset.

Low will, low skill

When driving a sales transformation, rebuilding a sales team or restructuring, it is not uncommon to find a group of employees that fall into this category. Also, sometimes new starters who are still learning the ropes might drop here as they may be too afraid to ask for help. This group will need a lot more direction, training and support, especially if they are new hires. The coach needs to be honest with them, tell them what is required, tell and show them how to do it, and if they are unable to make the step change and mindset change then unfortunately they will need to be let go.

Do I need to tell people what to do?

The challenge when driving teams for performance is the balance between:

Command and control	telling people what to do, managing them through the numbers
Empowering people	allowing them to use initiative and delegate the responsibility.

There is a balance between the two and as we look at coaching for high performance and driving the right behaviours, we need to choose the style according to the person and the situation at hand. The model highlighted below is based on three different models:

Ken Blanchard's Situational Leadership model, the Conscious Competency Model attributed to Noel Burch, and the Johari Window created by Joseph Luft and Harrington Ingham (Jo and Hari).

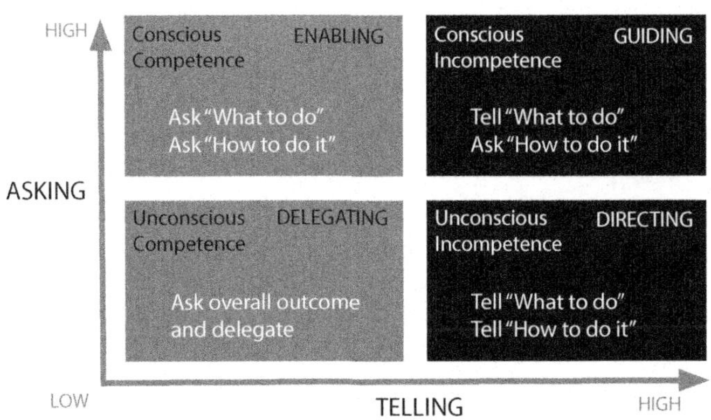

This model is extremely useful when managing salespeople as many of them learn their trade through trial and error and have certain things they do in a totally unconscious manner. If you were to ask them what they do and why they do it, they are often unable to answer with any definitive response.

Unconscious incompetence

This is an interesting box when looking at salespeople. Unconscious means that people are unaware of what they are or are not doing. When observing your team and colleagues you may be able to spot some of the things that they do, or the absence of certain things, which put them into this category. The word 'incompetence' is not meant in a derogatory tone, it simply means that the person may not realise that they are not very good at a certain thing. Therefore they are unconsciously incompetent.

It is in this position where you will need to tell the person what to do and tell them how to do it. Don't confuse this with low will as described in the skill/will matrix, but do expect the person to not always agree with what you are saying. If you want them to see what you see, be prepared to provide evidence, and hold the mirror up for them to reflect. To work with this person and to assist them to improve you need to adopt a more directive style, providing more direction, training, teaching and support.

Conscious incompetence

Moving onward from being unconsciously incompetent, this stage is more useful as the person you are working with is aware of the skills and behaviours but are also aware that they have not yet mastered them, therefore consciously incompetent. This will usually mean that the person is open to learn and open to feedback. The term guiding is used here to demonstrate the role the coach would take in providing direction and support.

In this position you will still utilise a more tell approach on what they should do, but then move to a questioning style by asking them how they think they would go about doing it. This provides a combination of support and challenge in the conversation where you are allowing the person to determine ways of moving forward with good guidance from the coach.

Conscious competence
This position on the chart is for those people who know what to do and can do it. The key to this box is that the person is consciously aware of the skill and capability and is using it when necessary. A lot of time for us at Salecology is spent trying to help people be aware of what they are doing, rather than just doing it unconsciously. If you do it unconsciously then you won't know when you do or don't do it, thus it is hard to know if you are skipping aspects on those days when things are not going to plan.

Working with people in this box, your coaching style changes to a highly supportive role rather than a directive one. It is at this point where you enable the person to find their own way. It is best in this situation to provide insight that will help the person see things differently and prompt reflection on what went well and what could have been better. In essence, ask 'What they think they should do' and ask 'How they think they will do it'.

Unconscious competence
The top performers seem to just do the right things in an unconscious manner. These could be skills and habits formed over the years or they have some personality traits that just work. There are two elements to consider for this. As it is an unconscious action, you seller won't be aware of what they do, and therefore won't know when they are not doing it. Therefore, if you have some salespeople that on some days are smashing their targets and other days things just don't seem to be going their way, it could be because they have stopped doing something they normally do. Because it is an unconscious behaviour they won't be aware of it.

As a coach for these performers, you will need to raise their level of consciousness on the particular behaviour and point out to them what is being missed and 'as if by magic' they will be back performing again.

Pulling information from these groups is the best way to manage and coach them. They have a clear skill and natural ability to do the task so helping them spot small incremental increases will be highly valuable. If possible, moving them back into the conscious competency area will enable them to repeat their success, consciously!

Focus on the behaviour – not the results

When coaching for behaviour change you should be focused more on what people are doing and their activities that lead to the output, not the output itself. For example, if the salesperson has poor conversion rates it isn't simply a question of forcing them to up the amount of deals in the pipeline. Look at the areas where the behaviour is causing the problem and fix the cause not the symptom.

One of the aspects that works well is to go back to the sales process that we discussed in the previous chapter and look at the behaviours that contribute to the outcomes. When coaching and driving behaviours consider how to assist the salesperson spot what is going well and what they have missed.

Sales observations

Let me show you an example. Below is an extract of a sales observation form.

Sales Observation — Salecology®

Sales Person:		Date:	
Observer Name:		Dept:	

Scoring Scale: 5 = **Exceptional** - exceeded all expectations, 4 = **Great** - exceeded some expectations, 3 = **Good** - met all expectations, 2 = **Needs Development** - some but not all expectations met, 1 = **Below Expectations** - did not meet expectations

Connect	Undertakes proper background research	1 2 3 4 5
	Opens call in a friendly and appropriate manner	1 2 3 4 5
	Uses IPS to engage with the customer	1 2 3 4 5
	Uses Non / Verbal cues to engage	1 2 3 4 5
	Builds rapport - uses matching or mirroring	1 2 3 4 5
	Comments	Score - Connect
Explore	Uses Problem and Negative Impact questions to explore problems	1 2 3 4 5
	Uses Value and Positive Impact questions to build needs	1 2 3 4 5
	Explores decision making process, key stakeholders and timescale	1 2 3 4 5
	Uses active listening	1 2 3 4 5
	Uses customers language and style to build rapport	1 2 3 4 5
	Comments	Score - Explore

Focusing on behaviour, and coaching around it, is much more than a tick box, did you do this, did you do that, etc. Instead focus on what worked well and what could be improved. The example above is an extract of a sales observation form looking at ten behaviours within a sales call, five behaviours for connecting with customers and five behaviours for exploring customers' wants and needs. The focus here isn't did they do it or not, it is how well did they do it. The score system in this example is 1 to 5 where 1 is well below expectation, 5 is exceptional, with a 3 being met expectations. This gives the coach and coachee something to work on.

1 – Below expectations
A score of 1 in this example might be I didn't see you do it, rather than you can't do it, i.e. I didn't see it in that sales call. This is useful to raise awareness for the individual about things they think they did vs what they actually did.

2 – Needs development
This score is the most useful, it says that you did demonstrate some of this behaviour but it needs some work.

3 – Good – meets expectations
The core programme here is to get the team as a whole to a 3, i.e. you demonstrated the behaviour like we would expect and used it well in the sales call.

4 – Great – exceeded expectation
When people exhibited strong use of a behaviour it is important to recognise it and show them that they did well and therefore separates good from great.

5 – Exceptional – exceeded all expectations
Some of the sales team will demonstrate best practice in areas of the sales behaviour and you will want to hold them up as a glorious example of the different aspects. Consider a 5 score as something you would want to film and send off for an award.

The challenge with managers and salespeople is that they are used to trying to get full marks on everything and utilising the form above they feel like they should be giving everyone 4s or 5s. Remember the idea behind 4s and 5s is to give everyone the chance to stretch themselves and go beyond. It isn't for everyone to be exceptional at ten different behaviours. If they were, we should be focused on different behaviours not the ones on the list.

Utilising observation forms and providing good coaching and feedback will enable you to differentiate the 'know what to do' and the 'able to do it'. If you can record the sales call, then listening to the call together and both of you completing the form will enable targeted conversations and development. You can look at the scores and pick one or two things to focus on and make the change on the next call.

Design a form that captures the behaviours you want to see across the sales call. The example above shows two aspects, connect and explore; consider the demonstrate aspects and gaining commitment stages and the behaviours you would want to hear and observe on a good call.

Positive reinforcement – not a sh!t sandwich!

Coaching conversations, especially from the old school of sales management, is usually summed up as a sh!t sandwich. Give them some good feedback (top layer of the sandwich) then tell them what was bad (the filling) and then finish with another good bit of feedback so they don't feel too bad (the other piece of bread). Everyone knows the sandwich and it doesn't work too well. It has evolved into some standard questions like:

- What went well?
- What didn't go so well?
- What would you do differently next time?

These questions can be useful when working with those who are happy with self-assessment and can critique themselves, but it can also bring the focus on choosing the wrong elements to work on. Take the sales observation form above; if asked what went well, it would be easy to select all those items that had good scores, what didn't go so well, pick all the items with low scores, what would you do differently – choose a couple of the low scores to work on.

Tweaking these questions to be more positive and focusing on the strengths can reap greater rewards and maintain the coachee's motivation:

- What went well?
- What would have made it even better?
- What could you do next time to improve it?

This tweak to the question will enable the coachee to focus on their strengths and pick some things that might be a good score already and play more on their strengths. Of course, as the coach you might need to bring in some additional pointers and focus their attention on certain things, but it is all in a positive atmosphere.

Stretch not stress

When coaching people and driving change and transformation in the sales team, consider how much people can take on and make changes. There is an adage that a little bit of stress is good for you, but for anyone that has ever suffered from stress, or knows someone who does, stress is a very dark and horrible place to be.

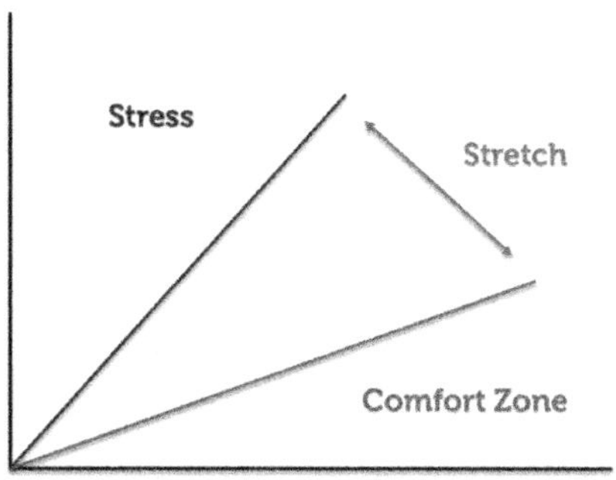

We saw this model earlier in the negotiation and objection-handling section. However, here I want to look at it from a change and coaching perspective.

The comfort zone is a happy place for people to be, it is somewhere where we are familiar with everything, we know the surroundings, we know what to do, we are safe, and everything is comfortable.

The stretch zone is where you come out of the comfort zone and try some new things and stretch yourselves. This is where learning happens when people try new things and new experiences.

The stress zone, or sometimes known as the panic zone, is where people start to feel anxious, nervous, out of control and it can affect their sleep, overall health and well-being.

The thing to know is that gap between comfort zone and stress (stretch) is different for everyone. If you are someone who always comes out of your comfort zone then your stretch area may be wider than those who have been doing the same thing for 30 years.

When coaching for performance and driving change in the team bear this in mind, even those people who have a wide stretch boundary can struggle to work on more than three behaviour changes at once. Therefore, when coaching make sure you pick between one or two things to focus on at any time. Change on many occasions works better when it is little and often, rather than big bang.

Coaching models

One of the most common coaching models is the GROW model. The GROW model was developed by a team of coaches led by Sir John Whitmore and colleagues in the late 1980s. The model was popularised in Whitmore's book *Coaching for Performance*, which was first published in 1992, and later by Max Landsberg in 1996, in *The Tao of Coaching*. The acronym GROW stands for Goal, Reality, Options and Will (or Way Forward), and it is a widely used coaching framework that helps coaches structure coaching conversations with clients to help them achieve their goals and reach their full potential.

The challenges with this model in a sales context is that it is often used incorrectly, or used at the wrong stage or time of coaching. The model is often used as a content-free coaching model. Content = free coaching is a type of coaching that focuses on the process of thinking and problem-solving rather than on the content or specific details of the problem. It is a non-directive approach to coaching that encourages the coachee to explore their own thinking and find their own solutions.

GROW model

The model is therefore used as follows:

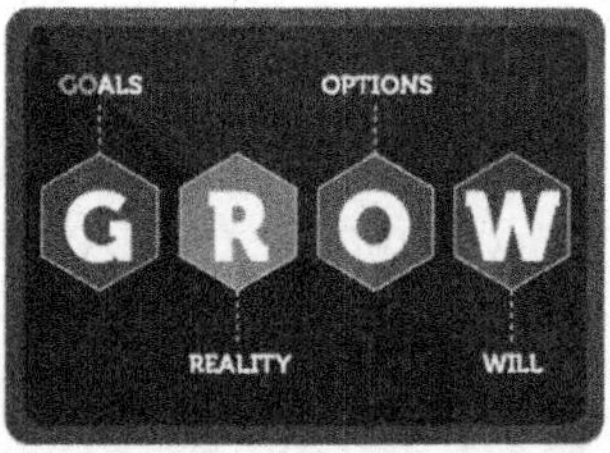

G – Goal   What are the goals they are working on? Agree the topic and specifics of the meeting. What are their objectives and goals they are working on?

R – Reality   What is the reality or current situation? Invite assessment of current performance or state, offer own view, prompt reflection. What have they tried?

O – Options   What could they do?

Invite suggestions, offer suggestions of actions to move towards the goal.

W – Will | What will they do? Make some choices and commit to action.

Content-free coaching is based on the belief that the coachee already has the knowledge and resources needed to find solutions to their problems. The coach's role is to facilitate the coachee's thinking process by asking open-ended questions, reflecting back what they hear, and exploring underlying assumptions and beliefs. It can be particularly effective in situations where the coachee is dealing with complex or sensitive issues and needs to explore their thinking in a safe and non-judgemental environment. The challenge here is that some coachees will be unconsciously or consciously incompetent and therefore will not have the answer to the problems.

Sales coaching is often anything but content-free! The manager is looking at the sales number, the sales performance to date and a host of different dashboard reports. The worst case I have seen of this in action by as a sales manager can be summed up with the following monologue:

G *What is your goal – to hit target*
R *The reality is that you are 15% behind*
O *The option is that you get back to the number or you're fired*
W *So what will you do? .... Get back on target, brilliant!*

Talk about motivational coaching!

In reality, the GROW model is useful for those quarterly, half yearly or annual appraisal meetings when you are taking time to reflect and set some longer term goals and aspirations. They can also work at the end of a day's sales accompaniment when you have had a debrief and get into some details about what to do over the coming weeks or month.

To use the GROW model in a better context, here are some suggestions to make it more appropriate.

Goals
As explained earlier, the coachees can't all be treated as if they know the answers to the questions. Asking salespeople off the bat, what areas are

you currently working on to develop your sales performance, will not get much traction, especially early into a sales transformation.

When discussing the goals and aspirations you may find it easier to utilise some of the call listening or sales observation feedbacks to provide insight into what they may need to work on. Pick certain aspects of the sales process and methodology to look for areas they might want to work on.

Reality

The reality check is an important part of the conversation. When you start asking questions about why they want to focus on that skill or behaviour you may find that it isn't really the goal at all.

For example:

Coach *What are you currently working on, or what would you like us to look at today?*

Coachee *I would like to look at my conversion rates and objection-handling.*

Coach *Sounds good, what makes you think you need to work on that?* (reality check)

Coachee *I get a lot of push back about price, and seem to get a lot of different objections.*

Coach *OK, and what have you tried already?*

Coachee *I am happy with the ARCing and FFF, but the customer still seems to stall.*

Coach *OK, remembering the training, price objections come from selling on features, and others come from selling on advantages, how much time do you spend on questions and uncovering needs?*

Coachee *Well customers tend to want to get straight into wanting me to demo the product so it's hard to start asking questions.*

As you can see from this initial conversation, the reality check has flagged up that the goal/topic isn't really the goal for the training session, it is actually questioning techniques and engaging the customer into the discovery part of the conversation.

Options
The options part of the conversation should be more than the coach listing out lots of ideas about what to do in this situation. Depending on the candidate, the coach should ask the coachee to go first in listing various things they could do to try and develop their skills in this area. The coach should look at three different parts in this section:

1. Prompt suggestions	what could they do, what ideas do they have
2. Offer suggestion	some ideas or alternatives
3. Enable insight	share some thoughts and ideas of what others have done

The idea of the options stage isn't to discuss the pros and cons of each idea, it is to create a long list of ideas of what the coachee could do to achieve their goals.

Will (way forward)
The final stage of the model is to get the coachee to commit to action. From the list, invite them to make a choice of which ones they are going to do and coach them around the decision making. Sometimes you may find that it is a simple, OK what shall we work on today, or what will you do over the next few weeks.

Be SMART

It never fails to surprise me how much time or effort people put into helping and coaching others but then leave the meeting having some sort of high-level agreement on what will happen next. It sounds something like: *'OK, great session, so you will focus more on your questioning skills over the next couple of weeks and we can take a look together in our next catch up.'* The problem here is that you haven't set the person up to be successful, they sort of have an idea of what they are going to do, but by asking some more questions and leading them through the thought process of what they will actually do, will be a much SMARTER way of concluding the coaching session.

SMART objectives are a framework for setting goals and objectives that was first introduced by George T. Doran in 1981 in an article published in *Management Review.* Doran's original intent was to provide a way to improve the process of setting objectives within organisations, but the framework has since been widely adopted by individuals and organisations around the world.

The SMART framework provides a structured approach to setting goals that is designed to ensure that they are clear, concise and achievable. The five key elements of SMART objectives are:

Specific: The objective should be clear and specific, with a defined outcome that is easy to understand. It should answer the questions of who, what, when, where and why.

Measurable: The objective should be measurable, with clear criteria for success that can be quantified or otherwise evaluated. This helps to ensure that progress towards the objective can be tracked and evaluated.

Achievable: The objective should be achievable, taking into account the resources, skills and knowledge required to achieve it. It should be challenging, but realistic and attainable within the given time frame.

Relevant: The objective should be relevant to the individuals, team, or organisation's overall goals and priorities. It should be aligned with the broader goals of the sales team, product or strategy and contribute to its overall success.

Time-bound: The objective should be time-bound, with a specific deadline or time frame for achievement. This helps to create a sense of urgency and accountability, and ensures that progress is tracked and evaluated over a specific period of time.

When helping your team member set themselves SMART goals, it isn't about writing them out using the acronym, it is for you as the coach to use the acronym as a framework to support and challenge their objective to ensure they are setting themselves up to succeed.

Some questions that will help you keep them smart:

Specific:

- What exactly are you going to do?
- Can you describe to me what you are going to do in clear and concise terms?
- How will you know when you have achieved your objective?

Measurable:

- How will you measure progress towards your objective?
- What metrics will you use to determine if you have achieved your goal?
- How will you know if you are making progress?

Achievable:

- What resources do you have available to help you achieve your objective?
- What potential obstacles or challenges could stop you?
- Is it realistic, given the time you have?

Relevant:

- How does your objective align with your broader goals and priorities?
- How will achieving this objective contribute to your overall success?
- What impact will achieving your objective have on others?

Time-bound:

- By when? What is the deadline for achieving your objective?
- How will you stay on track and ensure that you meet your deadline?
- Do you need to break down your objective into smaller, time-bound milestones?

These questions can help to guide the coachee through the process of making their objective SMART by encouraging them to think about the specific, measurable, achievable, relevant and time-bound aspects of their goal. By asking these types of questions, you can help the coachee to refine and clarify their objective, identify potential obstacles or challenges, and develop a concrete plan for achieving success.

Their success is your success

The final thing to say about coaching for high performance is that the challenge with being the sales manager and the coach is the difference between authority and influence. As the manager, you will potentially be targeted and rewarded on team performance, and therefore need each of your team members to perform and achieve their targets. If they don't hit the targets, then there is a good chance you won't receive your bonuses.

When they are not performing it can be difficult to hold yourself back from becoming directive and utilise authority to start dictating what needs to happen. Remember back to how different personalities act and behave under pressure and check your behaviour.

To be a great coach, you will need a strong self-awareness and emotional intelligence to understand the salesperson and how best to coach them to be the best version of themselves. It is not about you, it is about them!

Consider their Salecology colour and how they would best like to receive their coaching, feedback and motivation. Will they want it with everyone in an open plan office and call it coaching, or a private room for a 121 conversation? Do they want it formal or informal, structured or unstructured? Do they want to be praised and recognised out loud, or a personal note and congratulations?

Adjust your style accordingly to maximise the comfort level for you team member, and ensure they receive the right level of detail and engagement to get the most from the session.

Final Thoughts

We have shared several key factors throughout the book,

Part 1 – The Psychology of Selling
Part 2 – Salecology through the Sales Cycle
Part 3 – Building your Emotionally Intelligent Sales Organisation

These final few pages bring us back to the beginning and look at energy and where our focus comes from.

Everything around us and everything about us is energy. Our brains are these incredible supersonic muscles that know, and compute, more than we consciously realise. Before we even interact, I feel you, I sense you and my radar security system is making judgements whether I want to, or if it is safe to, interact with you. We enter into every single interaction with energy and intent. What determines how successful your conversations and sales are will be whether you are a warm, safe and trustworthy person to enter into interaction with (or whatever qualities the customer is looking for). Understanding whether you are the person that radiates good energy, or whether you are the energy vampire, is extremely important to your life, not only in your role in sales.

In long sales processes where you are working on deals for months on end, every touchpoint is energetically vital. Your industry, marketplace and target customers are what they are. You are no doubt constantly forming connections with customers that are not like you, and maybe you don't have much in common with them, and the start-up point is cold. These are the moments where all the ideas, tools and techniques that have been presented to you need to come alive. Your adaptability and capability to reduce the customers' mental barriers and influence their subconscious mind is fundamentally important.

Underpinning all that, is all about energy and intent.

Focus goes where energy flows

Throughout this book we have discussed the idea of building connections and utilising that relationship to allow the person to open up and share with you their wants, needs and desires; learning how to uncover drivers for change and helping them to see the value in the products and services you provide. Still there is so much more psychology that is available for you to engage with and look at the way you act and behave that can attract people.

Part of emotional intelligence is your energy. People that come into contact with you will get a certain 'vibe'. The moment people meet you, they will get a sense, a feeling and will judge you, sorry but it's true. That vibe can either make them feel good or give them an underlying, nagging feeling. It isn't a rational thing, it is something sat right inside their thalamus that we spoke about previously, in the friend or predator chapter.

Everyone likes to feel good! If you are the one that makes them feel good when they meet you, then they will remember it and will move towards you every time. If you have a strong positive energy, people pick up on it, you create a positive environment for people to be around and it will become anchored in their mind. The same rules apply if someone has a bad experience, or you are someone that makes them feel bad, that too becomes embedded in their mind and will bring back a flood of negative emotions when they are in your presence.

What makes you likeable?

We looked at different personalities and how to match and mirror, but there are some things that just make people likeable and attractive to others, and quoting Tony Robbins, "people like people like themselves, or who are like how they would like to be".

In general, there are several things that make people likeable:

Positive attitude	People are naturally drawn to those people who have a positive outlook on life. That optimism, seeing the good in other people and/or situations, tends to give

	people a good feeling and therefore makes someone more likeable.
Confidence	People who are confident and comfortable in their own skin tend to be more likeable because they exude a sense of security and reliability. Being self-assured, not arrogant, can create a sense of trust and respect.
Kindness	Showing kindness towards others, such as through acts of generosity, thoughtfulness or compassion, can make people feel appreciated and valued.
Empathy	Along similar lines to kindness, showing empathy towards others by listening to them, understanding their perspective and feelings, and offering support, can make people feel understood, relatable and able to connect on a deeper more meaningful level.
Sense of humour	People who have a good sense of humour and can make others laugh tend to be more likeable because they create positive emotions and a fun atmosphere.
Authentic	Being genuine and true to oneself is a highly attractive quality. People appreciate those who are honest, open and transparent.

This list is not too dissimilar to Dale Carnegie's book *How to Win Friends and Influence People*. For him, he listed five key things:

Showing genuine interest in others: people are naturally drawn to those who show an interest in them and their lives.

Being a good listener: being a good listener is essential to building strong relationships with others.

Using people's names: Carnegie believed that using someone's name can make them feel important and valued (although overplayed can come across ingenuine).

Giving sincere compliments: sincere compliments can boost people's self-esteem and make them feel appreciated.

Being positive and enthusiastic: Carnegie believed that having a positive attitude and showing enthusiasm can make people more attractive and likeable.

Carnegie's approach to becoming more likeable emphasised the importance of being genuine, showing interest in others, and treating people with respect and kindness. Overall, being likeable is about being someone who others want to be around, feel comfortable with, and enjoy spending time with. It's a combination of positive qualities that make people feel good about themselves and the world around them.

Storytelling

Storytelling has long been a powerful tool for communicating ideas and engaging audiences, and it's no different in the world of sales. It brings energy to a conversation as they help to create memorable, emotional and impactful sales engagement that build trust, differentiate products and lead to action. Whether you're selling a product or a service, incorporating storytelling into your sales strategy will help you connect with customers on a deeper more meaningful level. Paul Smith's *Sell with a Story* lists several key aspects which are important for salespeople to include when utilising storytelling, most importantly that stories are far more memorable than just facts and figures, as they engage both the logical and emotional parts of our brains, making them more impactful and memorable, i.e. when you tell a story that resonates with a customer's needs or pain points, that customer is more likely to remember the story (and the product or service being sold) long after the sales pitch is over.

We know that people make decisions based on emotions, not just logic. Telling a story that evokes emotions such as excitement, empathy or inspiration, the customer is more likely to become emotionally invested. This emotional connection can be a powerful motivator for the customer to take action, whether that's making a purchase or advancing the sale.

Stories also build trust. By sharing stories that demonstrate the salesperson's expertise, empathy and understanding of the customer's needs, the salesperson can build a rapport with the customer that goes beyond the immediate sale. This can lead to long-term relationships with customers that are based on trust and mutual respect.

Use metaphors and analogies

OK, back to school for some language training. OK, maybe not. But two things that are very powerful tools in selling is the use of metaphor and analogies.

Metaphors	A metaphor is a figure of speech that compares two things that are not alike in order to highlight their similarities. Metaphors often use phrases like 'is like' or 'is as' to make the comparison. For example, 'life is a journey' is a metaphor that compares the experience of living to the experience of traveling on a journey.
Analogies	An analogy is a comparison between two things that are alike in some way, in order to explain or illustrate something. Analogies are often used to explain complex or abstract ideas in terms that are more familiar to the audience. For example, explaining how a computer works by comparing it to a human brain is an analogy.

The power of using these in your sales approach, and in storytelling, is that they can be used to explain complex or abstract ideas in terms that are more familiar to the audience. When you listen to some people tell stories, or even in the words of songs, you will hear metaphors used a lot.

Think about the sales tools we often use, they are all conjured up with metaphors: sales funnel, elevator pitch, silver bullet, golden ticket and even the cherry on top! The use of metaphors makes things understandable and brings some sort of imagery to the discussion.

Analogies are also great at simplifying something that is complex but likening it to something else. You would have seen we have used quite a few analogies in this book, such as using computer references as an analogy to the brain. Using analogies to demonstrate differentiation is also a great way to help separate you from the competitor products. They can also be used as part of the reframing process in objection-handling.

User cases

Much like an analogy, sharing past experiences such as user case examples brings more practical examples of how people have used the product or service. These can often be shared during a story tell, or obviously shared during conversations to bring the application to life. This brings strong grounded energy into the narrative and continues to build trust and appreciation for you bringing the story.

Beliefs and values

The bottom line (metaphor used intentionally) in terms of energy flow and focus comes down to your personality, beliefs and values.

We talked about positive energy, storytelling and sharing experiences but based on what you believe, your energy will be focused on the things that you feel are important. As an example, if your attitude is about pile it high, sell it cheap, and you believe that is what people want, your energy and focus won't be on premium service, quality shop fittings and the experience, it will be on low price, low cost, no frills. That doesn't mean you don't care about good service, it is just the energy and focus will be in different areas.

Your role preference

We saw in the colourful personality section in Part 1 of the book that the different colours like to be sold in different ways. Well, depending on your colour preferences your energy will also be focused in different parts of the sales cycle.

Let's take a look at the Orange Salecology colour preference as an example. As a salesperson, the things you will love are the customer interaction, the engagement, the creativity of the role and so on. When you are doing Orange types of activity then it gives you energy. You are, figuratively speaking, in your element (sunshine).

Also discussed in that chapter was about the opposites. From an Orange perspective, you opposite colour is the Blue energy. Therefore, tasks that require more quiet time, working on your own and getting on with the paperwork and CRM updates, etc. will drain your energy, and therefore you will find yourself putting these off. For the Orange preference this often plays out such as a great meeting, great opportunity, but for some reason the proposal document takes considerably longer to send across to the customer as other Orange types of activity become prioritised.

The opposite is also true, a Blue preference will be strongly focused on the introverted thinking aspects of the role, prioritising building game plans, campaigns, and will enjoy being the subject matter expert, being the problem solver and building the solutions. Those things give energy and therefore become a focus, whereas the Orange energy tasks such as engaging in chit-chat, heavy customer interaction (not task-focused) can be quite draining and therefore tend to be put off or replaced with a preference for email.

But your beliefs and values also impact their behaviour and approach to sales.

Beliefs are ideas or convictions that a person holds to be true, often based on personal experiences, culture or upbringing. Beliefs can shape a person's worldview, influencing how they think, feel and behave in different situations.

Values, on the other hand, are a person's fundamental beliefs about what is important or desirable in life. Values can include things like honesty, respect, fairness or loyalty, and can shape a person's attitudes, behaviours and priorities.

Both beliefs and values can have a significant impact on your decision making, motivation and behaviour, and can influence how you approach different aspects of your life, including your career, relationships and personal development. In sales, understanding a person's beliefs and values can be important for tailoring a sales pitch and building a rapport with the customer, and they also play a significant role in shaping the way that you approach your role.

Sales style

You sales style is largely influenced by your beliefs about what works in sales and what doesn't. For example, a salesperson who believes that being aggressive and persistent is the key to success may adopt a more confrontational sales style, while a salesperson who believes in building relationships and trust may adopt a more consultative sales style. These beliefs can also impact a salesperson's communication style, including their tone of voice, body language and word choice. We discussed in the early chapter of the book the history of selling, and it is those early formative years in your sales career that definitely shape some of your beliefs about what works and doesn't work, and of course that will be a driver in the style which you adopt today.

Sales focus

We discussed this in the personality paragraph earlier but when we bring values into play as well, a person who values honesty and transparency may focus on building trust with the customer and providing accurate information, while a person who values achieving sales targets may focus more on closing deals quickly. Additionally, a salesperson's beliefs about the value and benefits of the product or service they are selling can also impact their focus, as they may be more motivated to sell a product they truly believe in. It is your values that will determine how much time you are prepared to spend in different aspects of the role.

Customer relationships

Beliefs and values can also impact your approach to building relationships with customers. For example, those who value empathy and understanding may take a more customer-centric approach, focusing on understanding the customer's needs and pain points and tailoring their sales pitch accordingly. On the other hand, a salesperson who values efficiency and productivity may be more focused on closing deals quickly, potentially at the expense of building long-term relationships with customers.

Hence the idea of having those who are focused on opening doors and warming up leads, different roles for closing the deal, and those who are more account managers. Hunters and farmers is the metaphor. We also see this play out in terms of the energy focus on whether people quickly ascertain pain points and needs, and those who drill down. There is a balance between trying to help the customer vs trying to close a sale.

Defining sales success

How do you define sales success? I don’t mean how does your manager or company define it, but how do you define success? Those whose values focus on building relationships and providing value to customers may define success in terms of customer satisfaction and retention, while others who value achieving sales targets may define success in terms of the number of deals closed or revenue generated. These beliefs will impact your motivation and approach to achieving your sales goals and how you go about achieving them.

In the world of tough competition where it is incredibly hard to differentiate your product and services, your way to join the top performers is to incorporate **Salecology** into your behaviour, language and interaction patterns. Change your approach today and start winning!

Now go and unleash your Sales SuperPower!

Want More?

We at Salecology can help you and your organisation to bring these skills to life and help you win more, earn more and achieve more.

- Training and Key Notes
- Revenue and Sales Enablement
- Talent Development

Contact us today to speak with one of our Salecologists and chat about your requirement.

UK and International **+44 207 649 9959**

US and Americas **+1 646 652 0475**

Feel free to drop us an email **hello@salecology.com** or visit **www.salecology.com**

Thank you and even more for you.

Thank you for buying and reading this book. As a special thank you, please find below a QR code that will take you to our website and will offer you a **special discount** on completing a Salecology Profile, where you can learn what you preference colours actually are, you preferred selling style, which parts of the role your gravitate towards, shy away from and how to adjust your approach for your most difficult customer.

Plus you will also get access:

- Free resources
- Free training content
- Special discounts

Further Reading and Bibliography

Throughout the book we have discussed many topics and made references to different authors. Below are the references to those books and other articles and reading that you might find interesting on the different sections.

There is no such thing as a 'no brainer'

1. Wayne Payne, 1985, *A Study of Emotion: Developing Emotional Intelligence* (Cincinnati, OH: The Union Institute).
2. Willian Stern, 1914, *Intelligenzquotient,* 1912 original German edition by Stern, 1914 English translation by Whipple (Berlin: Zeitschrift für angewandte Psychologie).
3. Roger W Sperry, 1967, *'Split-brain Approach to Learning Problems.'* In The Neurosciences: A Study Program (New York: Rockefeller University Press).
4. Daniel Goleman, 2006, *Emotional Intelligence - Why it can matter more than IQ* (London: Bloomsbury Publishing)
5. Gerald Zaltman, 2016, *How Customers Think: Essential Insights Into the Mind of the Market* (Boston: Harvard Business School Press)

Friend, predator or potential lover

1. John Grinder & Richard Bander, 1975, *The Structure of Magic: A Book About Language and Therapy* (California, Science and Behavior Books)
2. Eric Berne, 1957, *Ego states in psychotherapy.* (Washington: American journal of psychotherapy)
6. Eric Berne, 1958. *Transactional analysis: A new and effective method of group therapy.* (Washington: American Journal of Psychotherapy)
3. Mark Bowden, Tracey Thomson, 2019 *Truth & lies: what people are really thinking (First ed.).* (Toronto: HarperCollins Canada)
4. Chris Ciolii, 2020, *Beyond the handshake, how people greet each other around the world.* (Article AFAR.com)

Our colourful personalities

1. Carl Jung, 1921, *Psychological Types* (Zurich: Rascher Verlag)
2. Carl Jung, 1959, *The Archetypes and the Collective Unconscious* (New Jersey: Princeton University Press)
3. Ethan Boldt, 2009, *Psychology of the mailer* (Philadelphia: North American Publishing)

Shut up and listen!

1. Arthur Carmuzzi, 2017, *Architects of Extraordinary Team Culture: 5 Secrets from The Ancient Pyramids* (Kuala Lumpur, Malaysia: KV Publishing)
2. Tony Robbins. 2020, *Awaken the Giant Within: How to Take Immediate Control of Your Mental, Emotional, Physical and Financial Destiny!* (New York: Simon & Schuster)
3. Albert Mehrabian, 1971, *Silent Messages* (Belmont, CA, Wadsworth Publishing Company)
4. John Grinder & Richard Bander, 1975, *The Structure of Magic: A Book About Language and Therapy* (California, Science and Behavior Books)
5. Stephen Covey, 2013, *The 7 Habits of Highly Effective People: Powerful Lessons in Personal Change.* (New York: Free Press)
6. Deborah Tannen, 2017, *You Just Don't Understand: Women and Men in Conversation.* (New York: William Morrow)
7. Marshall Rosenberg, 2015, *Nonviolent Communication: A Language of Life.* (Encinitas, CA: PuddleDancer Press)
8. John Medina, 2014, Brain Rules: 12 Principles for Surviving and Thriving at Work, Home, and School. (Seattle: Pear Press)
9. Paul MacLean, 2001, *"The Triune Brain, Emotion, and Scientific Bias." In The Emergence of Neuroscience in the Twentieth Century,* (edited by Stanley Finger, Franck Stahnisch, and François Boller, 219-232. New York: Springer, 2001).

Let's talk

1. Francis J. Aguilar, 1967, *Scanning the Business Environment.* (New York: Macmillan)
2. Robert B Miller and Stephen E. Heiman, 1985, Strategic *Selling: The Unique Sales System Proven Successful by America's Best Companies.* (New York: Warner Books)

3. Neil Rackham, 1988, *SPIN Selling*. (New York: McGraw-Hill)
4. Oren Klaff, 2011 *Pitch Anything: An Innovative Method for Presenting, Persuading, and Winning the Deal* (New York: McGraw-Hill Education,)
5. Chris Westfall, 2017, *The New Elevator Pitch: The Definitive Guide to Persuasive Communication in the Digital Age* (Dallas, Tx: BenBella Books)
6. Terri L. Sjodin, 2012, *Small Message, Big Impact: The Elevator Speech Effect* (Greenleaf Book Group Press)
7. Brent Dixon and Matthew Adamson, 2011, *The Challenger Sale: Taking Control of the Customer Conversation*. (New York: Penguin Group).

Lead the customer to the solution

1. Stephen Covey, 2013, *The 7 Habits of Highly Effective People: Powerful Lessons in Personal Change*. (New York: Free Press)
2. Claude Hopkins, 1966. *Scientific Advertising*. (New York: Crown Publishers, Original work published 1923)
3. Tom Hopkins, 2005. *How to Master the Art of Selling*. (New York: Warner Books)
4. Michael T Bosworth, 2015, *Solution Selling: Creating Buyers in Difficult Selling Markets*. (New York: McGraw-Hill)
5. Daniel Kahneman and Amos Tversky, 1979. *Prospect theory: An analysis of decision under risk*. (Econometrica, 47(2), 263-291)
6. Daniel Kahneman, 2013, *Thinking, Fast and Slow*. (New York: Farrar, Straus and Giroux)
7. Dan Ariely, 2010. *Predictably Irrational: The Hidden Forces That Shape Our Decisions*. (New York: HarperCollins Publishers)

Influence the mind through questions

1. Eric Loftus and Zanni, (1975). *Eyewitness testimony: The influence of the wording of a question*. (Bulletin of the Psychonomic Society, 5)
2. Neil Rackham, 1988, *SPIN Selling*. (New York: McGraw-Hill)
3. Mike Schultz and John Doerr, 2014, *Insight Selling: Surprising research on what sales winners do differently* (Hoboken, NJ: John Wiley & Sons, Inc.)
4. Gary Gaskell, 2018, *Value-Based Selling: How to Win Sales and Boost Profits by Understanding and Delivering Value*. (London, UK: Kogan Page)

Put the customer into a buying mindset

1. Derren Brown, 2017, *Tricks of the Mind.* (London: Transworld Digital)
2. Milton H. Erickson and Ernest L Rossi, 2006, *Hypnotherapy: An Exploratory Casebook.* (New York: CRC Press)

Adapt sales presentations to make sense

1. Richard Bandler and John Grinder, 2011, *Frogs into Princes: Neuro-linguistic programming.* (Moab, UT: Real People Press)
2. Raymond S. Nickerson, 2015, *Confirmation Bias: A Ubiquitous Phenomenon in Many Guises.* (New York: Psychology Press)
3. Cowan, N. 2001. *The magical number 4 in short-term memory: A reconsideration of mental storage capacity.* (Behavioral and Brain Sciences, 24(1), 87-114.)
4. Risen, J. L., & Gilovich, T. 2007. *Another look at why people are reluctant to exchange lottery tickets.* (Journal of Personality and Social Psychology, 93(1), 12-22.)

Negotiate the close

1. Zig Ziglar, (2004) *Secrets of Closing the Sale.* (Old Tappan, NJ: Revell)
2. Rosamund Stone, and Benjamin Zander. (2019) *The Art of Possibility.* (New York: Penguin Books)
3. Laura Whitworth, Karen Kimsey-House, and Henry Kimsey-House, 2018, *Co-Active Coaching.* (Boston: Nicholas Brealey)
4. Roger Fisher, William Ury, and Bruce Patton (2021) *Getting to Yes: Negotiating Agreement Without Giving In.* (New York: Penguin Books)
5. Jim Camp, 2002, *Start with No: the negotiation tools the Pro's don't want you to know.* (New York: Crown Business)
6. Chris Vos and Tahl Raz, 2016, *never split the difference: Negotiating as if your life depended on it.* (Random House, London).
7. Michael Morris, Peter Karrass and Russell Korobkin, 2015, *The new face of face-to-face communication: How videoconference is changing negotiation.* (Academy of Management Perspectives, 29(3), 364-380.)

Have I got the right salespeople?

1. Susanna Urbina, 2014, *Essentials of Psychological Testing.* (Hoboken, NJ: John Wiley & Sons)
2. Gary Groth-Marnat, 2016, *Handbook of Psychological Assessment.* (Hoboken, NJ: John Wiley & Sons)
3. Raymond B Cattell and Alan K. S. Cattell, 2017, *Measuring Intelligence with the Culture Fair Tests.* (Champaign, IL: Institute for Personality and Ability Testing)

How do I build 'our way' of selling?

1. Adam Richardson, 2018, *The Customer Journey: How to Use Customer Journey Mapping to Improve Customer Experience.* (London: Kogan Page)
2. Aaron Ross and Marylou Tyler 2011, *Predictable Revenue: Turn Your Business Into a Sales Machine with the $100 Million Best Practices of Salesforce.com.* (Burlingame, CA: PebbleStorm, Inc)

How do I coach for high performance?

1. Max Landsberg, 2019, *The Tao of Coaching: Boost Your Effectiveness at Work by Inspiring and Developing Those Around You.* (London: Profile Books)
2. John Whitmore, 2017, *Coaching for Performance: GROWing Human Potential and Purpose - The Principles and Practice of Coaching and Leadership. 5th ed.,* (London: Nicholas Brealey Publishing)
3. Blanchard, Ken, Patricia Zigarmi, and Drea Zigarmi. 2013, *Leadership and the One Minute Manager: Increasing Effectiveness Through Situational Leadership. 2nd ed.,* (New York: William Morrow)
4. Mike Clayton, 2015, *The Conscious Competence Ladder: A Framework for Teaching and Learning.* (Scotts Valley, CA: Createspace Independent Publishing Platform)
5. Joseph Luft, and Harry Ingham (1955). The Johari window: A graphic model for interpersonal relations. University of California, Western Training Laboratory.
6. George T Doran, 1981, *There's a S.M.A.R.T. way to write management's goals and objectives (*Management Review, 70(11), 35-36.)

Focus goes where energy flows

1. Dale Carnegie 2021, *How to Win Friends and Influence People.* (New York: Simon & Schuster)
2. Paul Smith, 2016, *Sell with a Story: How to Capture Attention, Build Trust, and Close the Sale.* (New York: AMACOM)

Index

3 levels of listening 69-71, 103-105
3 Whys 77-79, 81, 96, 109
4 Parts of a Sale 48-55, 73
4Q Questioning 105-112
5P's of marketing 15
5 Types of Listening 65, 66
7/38/55 Rule 66, 67

A

ability tests - 162
accessing the subconscious mind 69-71
active listening 66, 71, 107, 151
adult to adult 40, 41 137
adversarial stance 147, 148
analogies 198, 199
and instead of but – 138, 139
aptitude 160-163
ARC – 140
Archetypes 45
Asking for help 152
Assessment centres 167
Auditory preference 127 -131, 143
Advantages 88, 89, 91, 138, 190
amygdala 33 140
archetypes 43, 44
assumptive listening 65
attentive listening 66

B

Background questions 85, 105, 106
Behavioural event interviews (BEI) 166
Benefit statements, 15, 83, 85, 89, 90, 92, 108, 109, 118
Beliefs 122, 123, 165, 200
blue personality 51-53,
    blue on a bad day 51,
    blue on a good day 51,
    blue in stretch / stress mode 145, 146
    emailing to a blue 57-61
    negotiating with a blue 148
    selling to blue 51, 52, 53
body language 27, 32-37, 48, 52, 66-68, 103, 115, 201
Brain functionality 19, 24-31, 102,103

Brain Operating System bOS 123-135
Audio preference. 127-131
Physical preference 131-135
Visual preference 124-127
Business Case – for change 109
Buying cycle 19, 73, 141, 172
Buyer Types 75-77
economic buyer 75, 76
managerial buyer 76
operational buyer 76
strategic buyer 75, 76
technical buyer 76
user buyer 76
buying mindset 114
Buyers tactics / tricks 155, 156

C

cadence 39 176
calibrated questions 150, 151
call to action 60, 61
capability (assessment) 161, 166-169, 177, 183
challenging the status quo 16,
champions 69, 110, 112
coaching 177-194
coaching models 188
Conscious competency 181-183
Johari window 181
Sales Observations 184-186
skill will matrix 179, 180
SMART objectives 191-193
Cognitive bias, 93 – 97, 123
colourful personalities 44-61,
communication being received 66
Competency 166, 167
competition 12- 16, 90, 146, 202
Conscious competency 181-183
Confirmation bias 123
Closing 60, 137, 202
Curious (be) 38
Customer journey 170, 171

D

Diagrammatical reasoning 162
Direct questions 100
Distinctive Selling Points 90
Distractions 41

E
Economic buyer 75, 76, 113
emails 57-61, 81,
  Call to action (CTA) 60, 61
  content 59, 60
  greetings 58, 59
  initial positioning statements, 80, 81
  Signing off 61
  subject line 57
emotional awareness 27
Emotional Brain 24, 26
emotional drivers / triggers 30, 62 -64, 69, 71, 104, 151, 196
Emotional Intelligence 25-31,
Emotional filter 105
empathy 29 60, 117, 119, 142 152, 153, 196, 197
Empowerment 181
Energy 195 196
Elevator pitch 80
evolution of sales 14-17
experience 159, 161, 167
Extroversion / extroverts 46, 47, 49, 56, 104, 164
Eye Movement 68

F
fast logic 70, 103
Features, Advantages, Benefits (FABs) 15, 25, 85, 86, 87-90
Feel, Felt, Found (FFF) 141
fight or flight 32, 33, 137,
filters interpreting communication 122
Financial crisis 16
FOMO, fear of missing out, 94, 95
four parts of a sale, 48-55, 73
Frame of reference 69
Framing 155, 158
friend, predator or potential lover 32

G
Gaining buy-in 118, 119
Get the no – 149, 150
green personality 53 -55
  emailing a green 57-61
  green on a bad day 53
  green on a good day 53
  negotiating with a green 148
  selling to green 53, 54, 55
  stretch / stress mode for a green 145, 146

greetings 32, 58
Grow model 188 - 191

H
Handshake (greetings) 32
high performance 159, 161, 177, 178
hypothetical questions 101
Hypnosis 116
Hypnotic Heartbeat 116-122, 142

I
Illusion of control 149
Impact questions 109-112, 119, 120
indifference 32,
industrial revolution 14
Initial Positioning Statements (IPS) 80-84
Insight 74
Intent 195, 196
Intellect 24, 25
Internet selling 16,17,
Interviews (recruitment) 165, 166
Introverts 47
IQ vs EQ 25
irrational brain 26, 30, 44, 85, 94

J K
Johari window 181
judgement 68, 87, 108, 195
Jungian theory 45
Knowledge, skills, behaviour 173, 174

L
Leading questions 99, 100
left brain right brain 24
likeable 196, 197
listening 15, 43, 62-69, 71, 103-105, 196, 197
logical brain 17, 24, 30, 72
Loss Aversion 93-97

M
Margin (reframing) 158
masks 45, 55
matching 35, 36, 37, 67, 68, 115, 140,
Metrics 112, 113
Metaphor 198
Methodology 170-174

mirroring 35, 36, 37, 67, 68, 115, 140,
motivation
customer 28, 62, 63,
sales person 164-168, 179, 201, 202
Multi-embedded questions 101, 102
Myers Briggs Type Indicator 163

N
Negotiation 137-158
Objections 138-143
Personality factors in negotiation 145-146
Problem solver stance 146, 147
Adversarial stance 147, 148
Calibrated questions 150
Price 154-158
Neurolinguistics 18, 20, 21, 24, 26,
neuroscience 18, 19, 98
NLP 26, 35, 122, 124,
norming group 163
numerical reasoning 162

O
Objections
General objections, 87, 89 , 138
Handling 140 – 144
Price objection 86, 88 138
Observations (sales coaching) 184-186
Open and closed questions 98, 99
Opening Statements 79-84
Opposite types 55, 56
orange personality 47-49
emailing to an orange 57-61
negotiation for orange 149
orange on a bad day 48
orange on a good day 48
orange overview 47
selling to orange 48, 49
stretch / stress mode for orange 145

P
Pacing and Leading 115, 116, 140
Pain Points 78, 85, 109, 174-176, 198, 202
Pain and Gain 91-93, 113, 174-176
parent - child 42, 43
passive listening 65
Performance predictors 159, 161, 168

Persona 45, 55
Personality test 163, 165
persuasion 18, 19, 80,
Pestel Analysis 74-75
Physical operating system 131- 135, 144
Playbooks and gameplans 174-176
Potential (assessing) 161-169
Potential lover 32
Power of 3 117, 130, 131, 142
Predator 32,
Price 113, 154, 155
Price Objections, 86, 88, 138, 154, 190
Probing questions 99, 100
Problem questions 107, 119
problem solver, 146-151
Psychology 18, 19
Psychometric tests 163

Q
Questions 91
Questioning techniques
- 4 Q questioning 105-112
- Background questions 105, 106
- Calibrated questions 150, 151
- Counter question 143
- Direct questions 100
- Hypothetical questions 101
- Impact questions 109-112, 119, 120
- Leading questions 99, 100
- Multi-embeded questions 101, 102
- Open and closed questions, 98, 99
- Probing questions 99, 100
- Problem questions 107, 119
- Reflective questions 99
- TED questions 100, 101
- Value questions 107-109, 120

R
rapport 31- 43, 98
- building rapport 34 - 40
- deep rapport 40, 41
- Matching and mirroring 35, 36, 37, 67, 68, 115, 140
- Mistakes when building rapport 40-43,
- Pacing and leading 115, 116, 140
- Wide rapport 40, 41

recruitment 161 - 167

red personality 49-51
emailing to red 57-61
negotiating with red 148
red on a bad day 50,
red on a good day 49
selling to red 50, 51
Red overview 49
stretch / stress mode for red 145
Reflective questions 99
Reframing, 142, 158
Relationship building 32, 202
reptilian brain 33 209
representational systems 122
Research 74-77
Resilience 164
Return on investment 112, 113

S

salecology colours 44-61
sales process 21, 73, 171-174, 184
Sales Style 200, 201
Sales transformation 159, 168, 181, 190
Selection 163, 164, 167
self awareness 27
self confidence 27
self regulation 27,
sh!t sandwich 186, 187
shut up and listen 62, 64,
situational leadership 181
skill will matrix 179 180
smart objectives 191-193
social listening 65
social skills 29
sociology 18, 20
Solution Heartbeat, 116-122, 142
solution selling 15, 25, 91
Standard deviation 162
Standard distribution curve 162
Status Quo Bias, 16, 30, 94, 96,
Storytelling, 41, 68 198 - 199
Stress 144-146, 187, 188
Stretch 144-146, 187, 188
subconscious mind 69, 70, 104, 105
Suspending belief 156

T
Target persona 176
Teach and tailor – 81, 82
Technical buyer 76
TED questions 100, 101
thalamus 33 194 209
three whys 77-79, 81, 96, 109
three levels of listening 69-71, 103-105
tonality 35, 66, 67 69, 71, 117 127 129, 135, 201
traits 28, 44, 144, 163, 164,
transactional analysis 42, 43
Triggers – 19, 31, 63, 71

U
Uncertainty 95, 115
Unique Selling Points (USPs) 90
Unquestionable truths 116
User buyer 76
User case 199

V
Values 122, 123, 164, 165, 200
Value based selling 107 -113
Value questions 107-109, 120
verbal communication 35, 37, 44, 66, 118
Value Propositions 12, 25, 26, 115, 143
verbal reasoning 162
visual preferences 32, 124-127, 143

W
well reasoned responses 70, 103, 104
Win win 146
What good / great looks like 159, 161
Why (three) 77-79, 81, 96, 109
Why the story is the story 70
work based drivers 63

TRICORN
BOOKS

Printed in Great Britain
by Amazon

38818960R00123